Secrets

from the

Wine Diva

Secrets

from the

Wine Diva

Tips on Buying,
Ordering & Enjoying Wine

Christine Ansbacher

Sterling Publishing Co., Inc.
New York

Library of Congress Cataloging-in-Publication Data Available

2 4 6 8 10 9 7 5 3 1

Published by Sterling Publishing Co., Inc.

387 Park Avenue South, New York, NY 10016

© 2006 by Christine Ansbacher

Distributed in Canada by Sterling Publishing

c/o Canadian Manda Group, 165 Dufferin Street

Toronto, Ontario, Canada M6K 3H6

Distributed in the United Kingdom by GMC Distribution Services

Castle Place, 166 High Street, Lewes, East Sussex, England BN7 1XU

Distributed in Australia by Capricorn Link (Australia) Pty. Ltd.

P.O. Box 704, Windsor, NSW 2756, Australia

Manufactured in the United States of America

Sterling ISBN-13: 978-1-4027-3036-8

ISBN-10: 1-4027-3036-5

For information about custom editions, special sales, premium and
corporate purchases, please contact Sterling Special Sales Department at
800-805-5489 or specialsales@sterlingpub.com

ACKNOWLEDGMENTS

Special thanks to the following people, all of whom have helped me by enjoying, learning, teaching, or sharing the world of wine:

First and foremost, deepest thanks to Bruce Johnson, my dear friend of 30 years, whose vast wine knowledge and wit made writing this book together so much easier and enjoyable. Bruce served as my valued partner on this project.

Denise Johnson, a senior communications executive and Bruce's wife, whose creative and marketing brilliance have helped shape my identity as the Wine Diva.

Robin Dellabough, of Lark Productions, who developed this project and injected an even greater sense of humor and charm via her edits, ultimately helping me find my Wine Diva voice.

Andy Martin, Patty Gift, Anne Barthel, Leigh Ann Ambrosi, Krista Margies, Becky Maines, and the entire team at Sterling Publishing, who have made my debut as an author a performance to remember.

Julie Trelstad, who believed in me from the first time we met, and whose work on this book proved vital.

Carol Edgar, a gifted wordsmith, who helped ensure the flow of this book and the consistency of my voice.

Randa Warren, DWS, CWE, my invaluable study mate while earning the two prestigious sets of initials after our names, who reviewed the finished manuscript to ensure its accuracy.

Linda Lawry, DWS, CWE, who tutored me in my wine studies for three years and singlehandedly pounded in the complex technical aspects I couldn't grasp in class, all the time providing great moral support.

Mary Ewing Mulligan, MW, of the International Wine Center in New York, who worked so hard to launch the three-tiered level of study from the prestigious London based Wine & Spirit Education Trust in the United States.

Last, but not least, the late Carter Burden, who gave me my first wine book and, in doing so, gave me the gift of a life's work and all the satisfaction that has come with it.

Contents

Secrets

from the

Wine Diva

*W*ine should be a laugh not a lecture.

*I*f you want to know how the soil and climate affect the taste of a wine, it's not in my book.

If you need an author to name wines she likes by *specific* producers from *specific* vintages that probably are not stocked in your store or are sold out, it's not in my book.

If you want flowery descriptions like "Syrah tastes like blueberries with a whiff of smoky bacon fat and freshly laid asphalt" in order to show off when describing a wine, it's not in my book.

But if the sheer enjoyment of drinking wine is your purpose, then this book is for you. It reveals immediately useful practical tips and secrets that will provide instant wine savvy. For example:

- Play TAG (temperature, aeration, glassware) to make a ten-dollar Cabernet taste like a thirty-dollar bottle. Go to pages 121–130 for the full scoop.

- Don't store your wine in the fridge. Its dry environment dries out the cork, allowing air to enter. The wine starts to deteriorate within two to three weeks. For my recommended alternatives, see page 135.

- No surgery is required to avoid red wine headaches. Just take an antihistamine, or try red wines with less tannin such as . . . Turn to page 164 to find out.

- To determine a fair price for a bottle of wine at a restaurant, figure on two and a half to three times retail. See page 96. Don't be embarrassed to ask the sommelier what the good deals are!

- Get out a stubborn cork with Cork Pop, a new gadget that removes a cork in one second flat. Or run the neck of the bottle under hot water so the glass temporarily expands and the cork easily slides out using your regular corkscrew. See page 131.

These are tips I share at wine tastings I do for corporations, cultural institutions, and nonprofit groups. My clients include icons like American Express, Merrill Lynch, Pfizer, and Wachovia, as well as cultural giants like the New York Philharmonic. Everyone, including novices, foodies, wine enthusiasts, and serious wine connoisseurs, has nodded, saying something like, "I learned something useful I didn't know before."

Say "hurray" or
"yay," it's great
to find a bargain.
So look for red Burgundies
like Santenay (san-ten-AY),
Marsannay (mar-san-AY),
Mercurey (Mur- cure-AY),
and Givry (jiv-RAY) on a
wine list.

I believe learning about wine should be fun, and I try to give my presentations a theatrical flair. I am called the Wine Diva because I am passionate about wine and eager to share that passion with others. Like any operatic diva, I have studied my art. In the ten years that I've been studying, reading, traveling, and conducting wine tastings, I have felt a distinct disconnect between what I have studied and what my audiences crave. So many wine books spend a lot of pages and your time talking about soils and climates, vine training systems and fermentation processes. My audiences just want to know how to select and enjoy a bottle of wine. I get questions such as, "What wine do you recommend to serve with Chinese food?" (Sparkling wine is my choice because—like beer—its refreshing bubbles douse the heat in these spicy dishes.) Or "How do I get a red wine spill out of my tablecloth?" (A product called Wine Away works magic, but in a pinch you can use a solution of water and high-acid items like lemon juice, white vinegar, or even zesty, unoaked white wines.)

As I made note of the questions regular folks want to know, my first thought was to find and recommend one or two of the many books on wine. But for the most part, books on wine enjoyment for the novice contain too much simplified technical text and aren't about just drinking the stuff. I couldn't find a consumer-centered book that was called something like *Just Enjoy Wine*.

So I decided to do something about it. *Secrets from the Wine Diva* is the result. It contains almost two hundred really practical tips, secrets, and shortcuts to help you buy, store, pair, and share wine. Absolutely no mention of soil, winemaking, appellation systems, or other vino babble!

Secrets from the Wine Diva is for wine drinkers, not wine thinkers. Time and again, I hear people say, "I love wine, but I don't know much about it" as if that's somehow a failing on their part. Confronted nearly every day with situations involving wine at restaurants, at home, or at the store, they react with apprehension or even fear: "Was that a smirk I saw on the sommelier's face as I made my wine selection?" . . . "I am tempted to try German wines but there is no way I can pronounce the name on the bottle. Oh God, I'm not even sure I can read the gothic typeface."

Secrets from the Wine Diva provides straightforward and immediately useful advice on topics such as why you should put your red wine in an ice bucket for ten minutes before pouring it, how to find real values on a wine list, or the best ways to stopper an opened bottle of wine so it's fresh three to four days later. I've organized it from your point of view—that is, the situations in which you face wine choices as you buy, store, and drink wine. Think of it as a private tutorial, not in all things wine-related, but only in things wine-enhancing.

On this delightful journey I will also give you a little perspective through entertaining anecdotes and tidbits that are part of wine's rich heritage. Wherever these bits of history illustrate a point, I have included them. For instance, why do we use the phrase "to make a toast"? It began with the custom of adding a piece of toasted bread (crouton) to a glass of wine in order to improve the flavor and to absorb the sediment that unavoidably floated in the glass.

If you pick up tips to solve real life wine dilemmas and remember one or two of the historical anecdotes, you will be hailed as a wine aficionado. You may not need to tell a wine-related anecdote, but once you've read my book you should feel prepared to choose the right wine, anytime, for any occasion, with aplomb, and most important you will feel comfortable in any situation involving wine. You will no longer have to endure the snobby wine store clerk, a sommelier's condescension, or the dismissive sniff of a pretentious colleague. Take away tedious memorization and studying from the subject of wine, and what do you have left? Good taste, good company, and the good life.

Cheers!

The Diva takes the Stage

"Christine, I think the cellar at the country house needs restocking. Don't spend more than fifty thousand dollars."

These instructions from my boss, a member of the Vanderbilt family, jump-started my journey into the fabulous world of wine. At the time, I was a personal assistant to this prominent New York social figure, businessman, philanthropist—and serious wine collector. Asked to maintain the quality of his 25,000-bottle cellar, I soon realized that my knowledge of wine was not up to the assigned task, so I began taking courses and attending wine tastings.

Sadly, my employer died suddenly in 1996, and I was left without a specific use for my wine savvy. But by then learning about wine and evaluating it at tastings had become a passion, so I decided to make it my profession. I plunged into grueling courses for wine professionals and eventually became a Certified Wine Educator (CWE). This certification requires an exceptional standard of academic knowledge and sensory tasting ability. At this writing there are only 180 CWEs in the U.S. Next, I earned an even more advanced wine degree from the Wine & Spirit Education Trust in London. Called the Diploma Wine & Spirits (DWS), it places me in a select circle with only seventy-five other U.S. wine professionals. In fact, only 20 percent of the students pass the rigorous written and blind tasting exams.

In addition to all this formal academic training, I've traveled to every major wine region in the world, walking the vineyards with the *vignerons* and tasting wines with the winemakers. I finally became what people call a "wine expert."

But what was I going to do with all this knowledge? I decided to share my education with others through wine tastings. My first tastings were like every one else's—a distillation (no pun intended) of my years of wine education. But I am, as many of my friends will attest, a natural showman. Very quickly, my tastings evolved from purely educational to pure entertainment—sabering off the top of a Champagne bottle (just as Napoleon's cavalry officers did to celebrate victory on the battlefield) has become my signature move and my best applause-getter. Then I follow it up by saying something like, "Hose down that fire in spicy foods with some bubbly. Just like beer, the bubbles act like firefighters to dampen the heat in your mouth!"

I became the "Wine Diva" at a wine event I did for the Metropolitan Opera Club, where my Champagne sabering and flair for the dramatic was called a "bravura" performance and some members dubbed me the "Wine Diva," the name I now use professionally. I think it reflects what I have become in the world of wine—opinionated, enthusiastic, and entertaining.

The saints come marching in to save you. Several affordable white Burgundies start with "Saint," like St-Aubin, St-Veran and St-Romain. You will generally find one of these "Saints" on the menu of an upscale restaurant.

My wholehearted goal in wine tastings, and now in this book, is to help you love wine as much as I've grown to love it. When I first began drinking wine I simply ordered it as a beverage to accompany a meal without giving it a lot of thought. Today, I treat picking a wine with the same attention as I do the food for a meal. For me, wine has morphed from a mere liquid into liquid gold.

To me it's not just a beverage or a drink you gulp down to quench your thirst—it's a very personal food choice. And to get you to love it even more, I invite you to take a fresh look at some conventional wine wisdom:

- Forget red wine with meat and white wine with fish. Be color-blind!

- Definitely seek out screw-capped wines!

- Throw salt in your ice bucket!

- You don't need to recork leftovers— Champagne can take care of itself.

The Wine Diva's Secret List

Once you've read the rest of this book, you should feel prepared to choose the right wine, anytime, for any occasion, with confidence. But I believe in instant gratification, so before you read another word I'm going to divulge a top-secret list of wines that will impress your friends and delight your palate.

To cut to the wine chase and expand your wine horizons beyond your favorites—Chardonnay, Sauvignon Blanc, Pinot Grigio, Pinot Noir, Merlot, and Cabernet Sauvignon—here is my cheat sheet for picking wines. The list includes some of my favorite interesting wines that are delicious with food and only cost between $10 and $20 a bottle.

In each category I've included at least two wines from the U.S. and six from overseas. My purpose is to coax you off the Cabernet and Chardonnay highway and onto more scenic back roads in four-wheel drive. You don't think twice about gambling on a $15 lipstick you've never tried or the latest golf ball, right? Think of it this way: Drinking the "same old, same old" in front of clients, colleagues, or a date doesn't set you apart from the crowd cruising on the highway. But when you order an unusual wine from my list on the following pages, all kinds of wonderful moments can result. When my husband, Max, was entertaining clients at an Italian restaurant, he remembered my list and ordered the Fiano. The waiter complimented him in front of the group, saying, "Most Americans can only order Pinot Grigio, but you've just picked one of Italy's greatest white wines. Bravo." Another time a client said he liked really big red wines. Although Max knew exactly which wine would wow his client, he couldn't remember its precise name. So he just asked the waiter for a red wine that sounded like "Bad Becky" from South America. (The waiter produced Malbec from Argentina.) Max's client said, "Gee, you must really know a lot about wine." Max doesn't, but he knows to use my memory triggers if he can't remember the name of a wine. So can you!

It takes a village. Remember that Burgundy is a veritable mosaic of tiny villages, and one area's wines are Macon-Villages (Mack-ON vill-Azh). These wines will generally cost less than the "Saints."

I've included the memory triggers that will help you remember each wine when you're caught in a wine shop or restaurant emergency moment, as well as the phonetic pronunciations in case you don't speak three foreign languages.

A Note on the Price of Pleasure

I am a great believer in trusting your own taste when picking a wine for every day or for a special occasion. I happen to think that finding a bottle of excellent quality at a moderate price is one of life's triumphs.

But there are times when a bit of splurging is called for. It may not be a wedding or an anniversary, but rather a rare gathering of friends who enjoy and appreciate wine. My cellar has mostly moderately priced wines with a few treasures among them. I save these for people who will love them as much as I do. I wouldn't invite people who consider gangsta rap their favorite music to hear Yo Yo Ma play the cello in my living room if I were lucky enough to have him.

Here are a few of my personal pricing principles:

8 White Wines	Pronunciation	Memory Trigger	Origin
Sancerre	sahn-SAYR	Sincere	France (Loire Valley) *made from Sauvignon Blanc*
Chablis	sha-BLEE	Shabby	France (Burgundy) *made from Chardonnay*
Riesling	REE-sling	Wrestling	France (Alsace), Germany, Australia, New York, California, and South Africa
Albariño	all-bar-EEN-yo	Al Pacino	Spain (Rias Baixas in Galicia)
Fiano	fee-AAH-no	Piano	Italy (Campania)
Arneis	are-NASE	Our Niece	Italy (Piedmont)
Viognier	VEE-ohn-yea	Virgin Air	California
Pinot Gris	PEE-no-grese	It's No Grease	Oregon and France (Alsace)

1. Just as you pair foods and wines, pair wines with guests (this is the casting pearls before swine rule). The flip side of this rule is that there is no one who deserves that special bottle more than you do . . . don't wait forever to open that great old wine.

2. If you can tell the difference, pay the difference. You can certainly tell the difference when you bite into a more expensive prime-aged steak from the corner butcher versus a regular supermarket cut. Why not pay more for a wine that you know firsthand gives you greater pleasure? We always take more sips of wine than we do actual bites of food, so the wine becomes an even more important food choice, and one that you shouldn't skimp on.

8 Red Wines	Pronunciation	Memory Trigger	Origin
Bourgeuil	bore-GOY	Boy Oh Boy	France (Loire Valley) made from Cabernet Franc
Cabernet Franc	CAB-er-nay-FRANK	Cabaret Frank	California
Crozes-Hermitage	crows-HER-me-taj	Crows in a Hermitage	France (Rhône Valley) made from Syrah
Côtes du Rhone	coat-do-ROAN	Goats do Roam	France (Rhône Valley)
Barbera	bar-BEAR-ah	Barbara	Italy (Piedmont)
Tempranillo	temp-rah-KNEE-yo	Temperamental	Spain (Ribera del Duero) Spain's answer to Cabernet
Malbec	mahl-BECK	Bad Becky	Argentina
Sangiovese	san-geo-VAY-say	Gee, They Say	California and Italy called Chianti in Tuscany

3. Have you ever bought a gift from Tiffany's just so your recipient could see the blue box? There are those times when status counts, especially if the person or persons will think it is thoughtful as opposed to merely extravagant. If you know that your friend has a thing for Jordan Cabernet, then by all means buy it as a gift! Just as you might feel more comfortable spending more for a designer shirt with the prestigious logo showing, so too should you feel comfortable spending more on a bottle that has a great reputation or is scarce—even if you haven't tried the wine. You trust the wine's reputation, the reviewer's comments, or its overall image to make you feel like you made a good choice.

A Final Thought

The only critic you need to pay attention to is yourself. Whatever I, or any other wine writer, think is not nearly as important as what you think—and drink. Buy what you like, enjoy it, and by all means don't worry about what anyone says is the "right" thing to drink.

Wine	Pronunciation	Memory Trigger	Origin
Muscadet sur lie	MUS-ka-day-SIR- lee	the Musketeer (or the muskrat) is surly	French white
Garnacha	gar-NAH-cha	gotcha!	Spanish red
Grüner Veltliner	groon-er-VELT-leen-er	the velvet crooner	Austrian white
Pinot Blanc	pee-no-BLANK	pee no more blanks	Alsatian white
Vermentino	Ver-men-TEE-no	vermin	Italian white
Zinfandel	ZIN-fan-dell	Zin is sin	California red
Rueda	roo-ED-ah	Randa	Spanish white

Buying
Wine

Buying wine in the United States can be simple—or simply an adventure. Some shops have very knowledgeable and helpful staff; others have no wine-savvy help whatsoever. In recent years, new venues for wine purchase have emerged. This chapter explains how to shop most effectively in:

- Supermarkets and superstores

- Wine shops

- Catalogues and online

- Auctions and charitable events

- Wineries

- Futures

Before you even set foot out your door to buy wine, ask yourself: What are you shopping for? Tonight's dinner? A present for your host this Saturday? Refilling the wine rack in the kitchen? Building a wine cellar? Each of these situations calls for a different shopping strategy.

Think of how you might go food shopping. Most of your needs can be met at the supermarket, but for some items, meat for instance, you might go to a favorite butcher who will not only select a particularly good cut but advise you on preparation. If it's a special occasion—a birthday, say—you probably go to a bakery and get a custom-decorated cake rather than grab one off the supermarket shelf. The same is true for wine. If you're picking up a bottle to go with spaghetti for the two of you after a hard day's work, making a special effort to find the best possible wine is not necessary. If company is coming to dinner, taking a little extra time at a reputable wine store is worthwhile. No matter what the situation, you can find the perfect place to buy wine. It's all a matter of knowing a few inside tips, which I am delighted to share with you.

Supermarkets and Superstores

When convenience and price are paramount and selection is less so, supermarkets are a fine option. If you are fortunate enough to live in an enlightened state where sales of wine are permitted in food stores (generally outside of the northeast), you simply pick up that bottle as you breeze through the wine section with a high degree of certainty that you will get a wine in good condition at a fair price. Because stock turnover in supermarkets is rapid, the danger that wine will be ruined by bad storage is minimal even if the bottles are stood upright on the shelf—normally a no-no. Because of their purchasing clout supermarkets generally buy well and adhere to minimal markups so bargains are plentiful. The supermarket offers you commercial brands that produce well-made wines with consistent taste from year to year.

The downside of buying wine in supermarkets is:

- Selection is often limited to wines named after the grape—think Chardonnay, Sauvignon Blanc, Pinot Noir, Merlot, and Cabernet Sauvignon

- Not a wide variety of different styles of wines

- No home delivery

- No discount if you buy a case

- No wine-savvy staff to ask for guidance

If you're unfortunate enough to live in one of the "dry" regions where supermarkets don't sell wine, you might want to skip over this next section.

Superstores such as Sam's Club, BJs, and Costco are extreme versions of supermarkets, the good and the not so good. Shopping at these "big box" stores, as they are known, can be a true treasure hunt. Their pricing not only varies between chains but within a chain. You are apt to find the same wine for a different price at one big box store as at another in the same chain.

Selection at big box stores is less limited than a regular supermarket and has more low- and high-end international choices, although it is still not vast. Stock turnover is high, so damaged wine

Calling All Supermarkets

 It has always amazed me that supermarkets have a unique merchandising opportunity that they seem to ignore: Pairing wines and foods. You may see some wine displayed in the meat section, but there is rarely if ever an attempt to give the shopper an idea of which wines would best suit those richly marbled New York strip steaks or the lamb roast (Cabernet Sauvignon, for instance, not Merlot) versus the more delicately flavored, lean filet mignon (Merlot, not Cabernet) let alone suggesting wines for the Pacific salmon in the fish section (Pinot Noir, rose Champagne, or perhaps a Chardonnay). For more detail on go-togethers see the chapter on Food and Wine pairing. This extra placement of wines would not only be a help to the customer but would also add to sales the way putting a stack of buns next to hot dogs, salsa next to chips, and steak sauce by the steaks all do. (Just a little public service announcement from the Wine Diva.)

is rare. A particular annoyance is that these superstores often deal in closeouts and special deals from wineries. That's great for prices, but chances are that if you go back to the store a few weeks after you got that great deal, the wine will no longer be in stock. My recommendation is if you see a bargain on a wine that you already know, buy it by the case. That said, Costco in particular can yield tremendous value if you're looking for high-end wine.

Here is my list of quality California, French, and Australian wines to snap up for those special occasions. Costco's 14 percent markup policy—as opposed to the usual 50 percent—makes these wines very well priced although they're not always available.

NAME	DESCRIPTION
Dom Perignon	Vintage Champagne
Veuve Cliquot Grand Dame	Top of the line Champagne
Leoville Barton	Red Bordeaux
Grand Puy Lacoste	Red Bordeaux
Gruaud Larose	Red Bordeaux
Château Ausone	Red Bordeaux
Penfold's Grange	Shiraz
Phelps Backus	California Cabernet
Cardinale	California Cabernet
Far Niente	California Cabernet
Phelps Insignia	California Meritage
Merryvale Profile	California Meritage
Rieussec	Sauternes, dessert wine
Suduiraut	Sauternes, dessert wine

Aside: Screw It?

You buy what you think is a "good" bottle of wine, bring it home, and find no cork. Did you get screw capped?

Cork plays a vital part in aging fine wines, but for everyday wines that are meant to be fresh, fruity, and consumed within the first year or two of their release—bring on the caps!

Screw caps do not mean a loss in quality. To the contrary, screw caps ensure quality. Think about it: Soft drinks and fizzy water all come in screw cap bottles because they keep the air out and the carbonation in. For wine, it's vital to keep the air out so the aromas and flavors stay alive. Initially, only non-European producers like Villa Maria, Fetzer, Bonny Doon, and Plumpjack used screw caps. Today European producers of premium wines such as Michel Laroche in Chablis, Georges Duboeuf in Beaujolais, Paul Blank in Alsace, and the Perrins in the Rhône Valley have introduced screw caps. I'm sure more

Case Studies

 Instead of experimenting in a restaurant where the markup is two to three times the cost of retail, the most cost-effective way to try new wines is to buy them at the wine store by the mixed case. Buy any twelve bottles and you are entitled to the case discount, usually 10 percent. Wine is more reasonable when purchased this way, and you don't lose sleep if several of your choices aren't keepers. I like to invite some of my wine-loving pals over to taste what I bought in the mixed case. You can taste more different wines that way and have a great time doing it!

You are on your way to becoming a true aficionado if you start buying a single wine by the case. The wine you buy by the case for your everyday drinking pleasure—your very own house red or white—means you won't have to run out to the wine shop every time you have dinner at home. When you can afford it, you can start buying case(s) of wines that improve with age and become more complex. If you can spare the space on the floor of your closet or in the basement for five or six years (assuming you don't have a wine cellar), this is a chance to buy great wine that in five years would be prohibitively expensive.

will follow their lead, which will be a cause for celebration. Screw caps mean the wine will always be vibrant and fruity, plus they are easy to open and reseal.

A Brief History of Cork

The wine-friendly properties of cork had been known since antiquity in ancient Greece, but were lost in Europe until the 1600s. Before then, wine enthusiasts used a variety of materials, including combinations of wood, leather, and fabric, to stop up their bottles. Cork, once developed, quickly became preferred over these stoppers because of its flexibility and ability to expand when wet.

Wine Shops

Wine shops—a.k.a. wine merchants, liquor stores, package stores, and bottle shops—all sell alcoholic beverages, and in today's market that more and more means wine. Distilled spirits sales as a percentage of all alcoholic beverage sales have been in decline for over twenty years, leaving beer and wine as the growth end of the business. Beer, which by volume is far and away the largest segment of the adult beverage market, is a low margin affair, so your neighborhood liquor store is morphing into a wine shop. For wine lovers that's a good thing, but not all wine shops are equal. Below are a few things to look for when choosing a wine store:

Storage

Until they are ready for their "opening" night, bottles are like the Wine Diva. They need their beauty sleep. Bottles should be either racked on their sides on the shelf or in cases on the floor. Bottles stood upright are subject to quality loss because corks dry out. Wines spotlighted for dramatic effects under bright lights are particularly to be avoided. Telltale signs of mistreatment during shipment or storage are:

- Dried or sticky wine residue on or near the cork or capsule (the plastic or metal covering over the cork) at the top of the bottle.

- Dried wine, which has oozed down the side of the bottle, perhaps even staining the label.

- Corks that may have been pushed out even the slightest amount from expansion inside the bottle—a sign that the wine has been exposed to extreme temperatures, either too hot or too cold.

Some other signs that a wine shop is not fully committed to its wine are bright lights and warm temperatures, neither of which makes for adequate wine storage.

Selection
A decent wine shop should be as worldly and diverse as the U.N., offering more to select from than the usual entries from California, France, Italy, Spain, and Australia. Look for representation from Germany, Austria, Argentina, Chile, South Africa, and New Zealand. (More about this later.)

Pricing
Contrary to popular opinion, dedicated wine shops are usually very good on price. Their business relies on high-volume buyers who are, in the main, educated customers and will not give repeat business to stores with generous markups. Case discounts are almost always available (usually 10 percent), and even bigger discounts on

selected items are common. Pricing policy is also the best way to avoid the precious wine boutique with high prices and serious attitude problems. With a little comparison shopping, you'll quickly spot the gougers. These houses of snootiness are the bane of the wine business, right up there with outrageous markups in certain restaurants.

Knowledgeable Salespeople

The number of stores with informed salespeople has increased dramatically in recent years. As wine drinking and wine appreciation have increased, so has the number of people who have made it their interest. Young people especially who have the passion, but not the money, to indulge their newfound love are now populating the ranks of wine store clerks and are usually happy to share their knowledge. A knowledgeable salesperson in a well-stocked wine store is to be treasured, cultivated, and supported. Unless you are a die-hard aficionado you will never have tasted as many wines as your wine shop clerk. Good wine stores

Market Value

 Most of us think a great-tasting wine has to be expensive, and some marketers take advantage of that. An old saying goes, "If you can't taste the difference, why pay the difference?" An inexpensive wine can taste just as wonderful as an expensive one, but you have to look harder to find these gems. A wine's high price is usually due to rarity, the quantity of that particular wine that is available for sale (in years with low-yield harvests when less wine is made). Piggybacking on regional reputations can jack up prices. For example Napa Valley wines—most are terrific, but certainly not all. High prices may be the result of sheer marketing moxie. One of the great pleasures in wine buying is what I call the Great Wine Hunt: Finding that terrific bottle of wine priced below its quality level. Like exotic, rare breeds, those wines are out there. Just keep buying and tasting.

hold regular tastings for their staff, so salespeople can probably describe the wines you're considering. If you shop with this salesperson regularly, he or she will get to know you and your tastes, can guide you to bargains, and encourage you to try new wines that fit your taste profile. It's like having your own personal shopper at Bloomingdale's. When I want to restock my cellar, I go to a guy named JR who is the manager at Garnet, a well-stocked wine store in Manhattan with terrific prices. My favorite everyday wine is always the last bottle I drank. Like most people, I fall in love so easily that I tend to restock on autopilot. I count on JR to nudge me when I fall into this lazy habit. When you've found your own favorite wine sales associate, don't be shy about providing details of that special meal you're planning. For each dish to be paired with a wine, describe the dish, its ingredients, and a sauce

Off-Road Treasure Hunting

 Don't you love discovering a work of art or furniture in an antique store, for a bargain price? The technique is the same for uncovering wine treasures. The best source is haunting shops that are off the beaten track. When you visit friends at their weekend house in a rural community, or stay with relatives in a small town, make it a point to check out the liquor store or wine shop. Oftentimes, their more expensive wines don't sell quickly and languish on a shelf because they are too pricey for the local folk. But you can sweep them up for the asking!

On one memorable trip to upstate New York I found some remarkable old Burgundies marked down to less than half their original price. "Are these wines sound?" I inquired. "Oh yes," I was told. "These old wines just don't sell around here." I gladly helped myself to all that the trunk of my car could hold. If you do find an apparent bargain, be sure that the bottles were lying on their side and not standing straight up or left on a shelf exposed to light. If these treasures have not been stored correctly, you've just got to keep wine hunting.

if you're serving one. Remember, the more input you give your wine seller, the more helpful he or she will be in helping select the right wine.

Many feeble geriatric monks chant voodoo nightly. Villages in Burgundy's "golden slope" that produce wines from Pinot Noir: Marsannay, Fixin, Gevry-Chambertin, Morey St-Denis, Chambolle-Musigny, Vougeot, Nuits St-George.

Once you've found your personal shopper, introduce yourself to the manager. Let the manager know three things: (1) that you are interested in wine, (2) would like to learn more, and (3) want to become a regular customer. Then develop a long-term relationship with either the manager or a sales assistant. Everyone's taste is different, and what one sales assistant finds fruity and soft may not please you. The solution is to try out the recommendations of several clerks until you find one whose taste is compatible with yours.

The goal is to get yourself on the store's insider trading list so that you'll be alerted when special wines are available. It's no different from having a regular salesperson at your favorite clothing store. You know this person will go out of their way to give you a heads-up when new merchandise is being put out, and even set aside items about to go on sale for you.

Markdown Madness

Buyer beware! Wine shops like to feature specials, which are sometimes actually loss leaders, wines the store makes little or no profit on just to attract business. The lure of a bargain always attracts shoppers. Wines that are on special and put out in baskets at the end of the aisles seem like a really good deal, but they could be marked down because the store owner knows these wines are not in good condition. Be aware that many of the wines in end aisle baskets have a shelf life of sorts. It's not stamped on the label like those on medications and certain foods, but young, inexpensive white wines should be enjoyed when they are fresh, within one to two years of the vintage date on the bottle. Young, inexpensive red wines can last up to three years—but Beaujolais Nouveau has a much shorter life span of about only six months. So if you see those inexpensive bottles marked down, it may be because they are approaching (or past) their peak of freshness.

Not all specials are good deals, but some are. Sometimes wines are marked down because they don't move—like wines from lesser known regions or wines that may be very good but weren't reviewed and therefore lacked enough buzz to catch on. They could be real bargains. I say if it's a discount, live dangerously and give it a try!

Wine Stores and Flavor Profile

Some traditional wine stores are reinventing themselves and pioneering a new approach. Best Cellars in New York organizes its wines by "flavor profiles" that help people figure out the style of wine they like. For example:

FIZZY
Sparkling wines from all over the world

WHITES
Fresh: crisp, citrusy, light-bodied white wines like Sauvignon Blanc, Muscadet, Pinot Grigio
Soft: medium-bodied white wines like Chardonnay from Chile and South Africa
Luscious: full-bodied white wines like Chardonnay from California and Australia

REDS
Juicy: light-bodied reds like Beaujolais Nouveau, Chinon
Smooth: medium-bodied reds, Pinot Noir and Shiraz, and some Merlot and Cabernet Sauvignon
Big: full-bodied reds like California Zinfandel, as well as some Shiraz, and Cabernet Sauvignon

SWEET
Dessert wines: Port and other sweet treats

This is a wonderful concept that I wish more specialty stores would follow.

Bad Bottle

The wine you bought tasted awful when you opened it at home. Can you return it and get your money back?

Almost always the answer is yes—for a wine that is not in good condition. A wine that you don't particularly will not be accepted back.

Prêt à Boire

 Go ahead and buy your clothes *prêt-à-porter* (ready-to-wear), but for heaven's sake don't buy your wine *prêt à boire* (ready to drink). I understand how tempting it is to buy a bottle of wine from the wine store's refrigerator on a steamy summer evening, but my advice is: Don't! (At least not unless you have totally forgotten your own anniversary and are late for dinner!)

Bottles of wine that have been refrigerated for extended periods are in low humidity environments that dry out their corks and let air in. Air causes wines to lose color and flavor. If for some reason you really need to buy a pre-chilled wine, buy a popular brand that sells faster and has spent less time in the cooler. If you buy a better wine, don't worry about the temperature. You can chill it to the right drinking temperature in minutes using my salt water tip in the Wine Service chapter on page 115.

The same rule of thumb applies in a restaurant. Save the recorked bottle and its remaining contents and return it, along with the receipt if you still have it. If your wine shop won't give you credit or another bottle of equal value, take your business elsewhere.

Online and Catalogue-Only Merchants

Shopping for wine online and/or through catalogues is a fairly new channel of commerce primarily because state and federal laws have generally prohibited direct sales of wines to consumers that bypass wholesalers and retailers. But a recent Supreme Court decision has opened the door to such direct sales, and online and catalogue sales are bound to increase significantly.

There are two types of online retail sites. One kind is a true wine merchant actually taking orders and shipping. It is this merchant category that will benefit the most from the recent court action. Prices on these online sites are reasonable but not necessarily better than what you can get at your local store. If you are in a state with a

State Stores

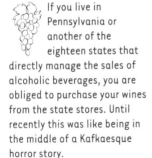
If you live in Pennsylvania or another of the eighteen states that directly manage the sales of alcoholic beverages, you are obliged to purchase your wines from the state stores. Until recently this was like being in the middle of a Kafkaesque horror story.

Those bad old days have given way to retail stores that look like privately operated ones, some of which have knowledgeable sales staff. In Pennsylvania, for instance, "superstores" have a good variety of wines and sales staff are quite well trained. Another advantage in the Pennsylvania system is that you can shop online, find any wine available anywhere in the state, and have it shipped to the state store nearest you! Just click on www.lcb.state.pa.us and shop till you drop.

competitive market (New York or California, for instance), you won't find many online bargains, but in states with high local taxes and little retail competition, online prices will be fair or even good. Their primary virtues are like any catalogue operation—convenience and choice.

The second kind of online site is essentially a search vehicle. The site does not sell wine but does tell you where to find any wine you might want, usually in great detail and specificity.

So what Internet sites does the Wine Diva like the best?

Search Engines

Wine-searcher.com and winealert.com are the leaders in wine-specific search engines, which, as well as being useful, can be a revelation. The difference in prices, particularly for keenly sought-after wines, is amazing. Individual wines routinely cost twice as much at the most expensive retailer as at the cheapest, and sometimes the variation can be even more for the exact same bottle. The modest subscription fees these search engines charge have paid me back many times over—I've pocketed tremendous savings thanks to the comparison pricing they provide.

The downside is that if you are shopping for many different styles of wines, you can go crazy trying to save yourself money. You may end up calling dozens of stores to find out that they don't have enough to meet your needs, or are sold out, which means more phone calls.

I recommend using Wine-searcher.com and winealert.com for special occasion wines or older vintages when you aren't buying in large quantities; you can find hugely different prices, and can therefore save a bundle.

Online and Catalogue Sellers

The convenience is seductive—shop at your leisure, any time of the day (or night), or phone and order wine delivered to your doorstep. Prices on wines are generally not great. The catalogue publisher knows the value of convenience and is charging for it. You should also check out the shipping and handling charges to make sure you are not surprised: Some are reasonable, some are not. Beware of online catalogue merchants who may try to make shipping and handling charges a profit center instead of a service to their customers. Many of these catalogues have obscure brands. This may be because they have found that secret vineyard with great values, or it may be that the brand is a private label of the publisher. While the wine may indeed be good, there is no way to comparison shop to see if the price is competitive.

If you prefer one-stop shopping, here are few of my favorite online catalogues from large, brick-and-mortar wine merchants:

Garnet Wine: www.garnetwine.com

Morrell & Company: www.morrellwine.com

Premier Cru: www.premiercru.net

Sam's Wines & Spirits: www.samswine.com

Sherry-Lehmann: www.sherry-lehmann.com

Wine Library: www.winelibrary.com

Zachys: www.zachys.com

Then there is an online catalogue from a company in Seattle with an eclectic collection of limited-production wines: www.garagistewine.com. Garagiste is an electronic catalogue only—there is no brick-and-mortar store from which to purchase wine.

Pros: They strive to introduce new, small, artisanal wine producers who make wine in limited quantities, as well as offer cellared wines purchased from properly stored collections. The range is staggering, ranging from a mix of high end, hard-to-find, cult wines to everyday table wines. While I judge their strengths to be in Italian and Australian wines, they do a good job including high and low end wines from around the world. Finally, their prices can't be beat! Why? They place the same margin on every wine they stock, regardless of a wine writer's score or limited availability. If a wine is reviewed after it's listed on their Web site the price doesn't change. They believe that wine reviews are a service provided by the author and not a license to increase prices. If a wine seems relatively inexpensive or expensive, it's based on their purchase price from the source, not their margins. Rarely can wines be bought less expensively anywhere else! So add Garagiste to your "favorites" folder on your Web browser.

Cons: Many brands will be unfamiliar to you because they are small producers hand-picked by Garagiste. While the wine may indeed be good, there is no way to comparison shop to see if their price is competitive. Since these small producers have a limited supply, when you get an e-mail you can't think about it very long; you have to make a snap decision and jump on the offer to get it, and then you may have to wait several months before you get the bottles. So it may be a case of hurry up and wait, which is frustrating.

They don't stock thousands of wines. In fact, they may have Burgundy one day and wines from Spain the next. Although there is no brick-and-mortar retail store, if you are in the Seattle area you can call their warehouse and make an appointment to wander through their "candy store."

Auctions and Charitable Events

There are auctions . . . and then there are auctions. Some auctions have a purely commercial purpose—that is, to sell wines that are not generally available or have a very limited supply, a private collection, for instance. Brick-and-mortar stores can also acquire private cellars that they advertise to their clients, but they generally do not match the breadth of wines offered at a commercial auction house such as Christie's, Sotheby's, or Bonhams & Butterfield. A few big retailers are exceptions: Acker Merrill, Morrell, The Chicago Wine Company, and Zachys. The customers at these auctions are usually well-informed collectors buying wines for their home cellars or restaurants who want to add some panache to their list.

The latest version of auction buying is on the Web. Some of the traditional houses above allow bidding by e-mail, but there are now pure Web-based auction sites. The best of these is www.winecommune.com on which individual sellers and buyers can buy, sell, or trade with no middleman taking a cut. It is the eBay of the wine world. The site makes a great effort to weed out unscrupulous sellers with overpriced offerings and poor service. Fees for selling wine on this site are quite modest—3 percent plus a small listing charge. Before you use any of these sites, check out the fees and commissions. The information in the chart below is a snapshot in time, not engraved in stone.

Sample Auction Fees

If you have been bitten by the wine bug and must have that '61 Mouton to fill out your collection, auctions are the place to look. But this is a game for pros and sophisticated collectors. A word of warning about any auctioned wines: Where had these wines been before they came to the block? How were they stored and under what conditions? Most auction houses can only vouch for where the wine was stored just prior to the sale. If you are about to make a substantial purchase, at least ask. If the auction house can give you some assurance, that's great, but if not, proceed with caution!

Auction House	Purchaser Premium	Seller Premium
Acker Merrill	17.5% +1% insurance	0% plus 2% insurance
Bonhams & Butterfield	10–15%	0–25% depending on $ value of consignment
The Chicago Wine Co.	0%	28%
Christie's	20–32%	8–20% depending on $ value of consignment
Morrell	17%	$25/case + 1%*
Sotheby's	17.5%	0–20% depending on $ value of consignment
Winebid.com	14%	11–18% depending on $ value of consignment
Winecommune.com	0%	3% plus small listing charge
Zachys	18%	0–10% depending on $ value of consignment

* On a case of wine where the low and high estimates range from $2,000 to $3,000, the mean is $2,500. One percent of that is $25. That 1 percent added to the $25 fee per case totals just $50 as the seller's premium.

Charity auctions are completely different. The idea is to raise money for some worthy cause with the added incentive to the buyer that his or her purchases are tax deductible. Add in an open bar that precedes the opening bids, and the inevitable result is wines selling for prices far above their real worth. By all means attend a charitable auction if you like the idea of giving to charity more than you care about the price and value.

Wineries

Visiting wineries is one of the more pleasurable outings I can think of. There may be no more beautiful way to spend a day than tasting your way through the Napa Valley, let alone a trip through Burgundy on a slow-moving barge or bicycle. Wine producers often offer informative guided tours of the winery, vineyards, and cellars to add to the experience. Restaurants in wine country are better on average and almost all of them have extensive lists of local wines. The principal advantage of buying wines direct from the winery is the opportunity to find out all about the wines at the source and taste them before you buy. Visiting small producers can be particularly heady as their wines may have limited distribution and may not reach the retailers or restaurants in your area. If this is the case, consider asking if you can be on their mailing list, and check to see if they can ship wine to your state. The Supreme Court decision in May 2005 easing restrictions on direct sales to consumers will, in many cases, make this kind of purchasing a bigger part of the business.

Don't expect wines bought directly from the source to be cheaper than at your local retail store. Wineries are well aware of the retail value of their products and, since they are offering samples (tastings), they have no need to cut price. They are also aware that the retailers who sell the vast percentage of their output would not be happy with cut-rate pricing at the winery. While winery listings are generally of the currently available products, it doesn't hurt to ask if there are any remainders from previous vintages or smaller lots not generally available.

For people who are armchair travelers, here are two Web sites that carry a huge number of California producers. These Web sites are direct-to-consumer marketing, so when you can't get to California, let California come to you via these sites, which include value brands and premium wines. They also offer the chance to join over fifty different wine clubs to receive ongoing monthly shipments, which saves you the time of going shopping each month. Certainly an easy way to stay stocked up.

www.hartwickandgrove.com

Hartwick and Grove were chosen by eleven of California's best wineries—including Robert Mondavi, Quintessa, Ravenswood, and Franciscan Oakville Estate—to serve as their official Internet retailer. Here you'll find a complete selection from these top-rated labels.

www.winetasting.com

This Web site provides "virtual tasting rooms" to fifty wineries, including top wine producers like Chalk Hill, Chateau Montelena, Far Niente, Joseph Phelps, and Trefethen. You use one shopping basket and one express checkout to cover all this ground.

Futures

The Bordeaux futures market is the IPO (initial public offering) for wines. It is not the only futures market, but it is the oldest and by far the most influential. Other futures markets, including the ones for California wines, represent a far smaller percentage of total sales for the vintage in question and barely impact the price you will see on retail shelves. The prices established in Bordeaux, however, allow wineries from other regions to index their prices, the theory being that what their wines can command is relative to what Bordeaux producers are getting. Futures is a game for the experienced and, like the stock market, is won by insiders. Run by the *negotiants* (shippers and wholesalers) in Bordeaux, the futures market largely determines the commercial prices for a just-concluded harvest—that is, two years or more before these wines will actually be on retail shelves. Release dates for wines are determined by individual wineries and not all are on the same schedule. Generally the lesser known and less expensive wines are released earlier, and the more expensive wines (Premier Grand Cru Classé) later.

The advantage of this system for buyers is twofold—to assure themselves of a supply of certain wines with a limited availability, and to lock in a purchase price in anticipation

Timing Is Everything

Avoid buying expensive wines during very hot months when the wines may have been shipped and stored in warm spaces. (You can't rely on their being handled properly in the distribution chain.) Far better to buy fast-selling, less costly brands during a heat wave because those wines have less chance to be ruined by heat damage. When the temperature drops to more moderate levels, you can safely resume buying more expensive wines.

that later prices will be higher. Whether this bet on availability and price is a good one or not depends on a mix of economic factors well beyond the knowledge of all but the most sophisticated players. You are buying on the basis of minimal and sometimes misleading information. Every vintage is hyped, sometimes with reason, sometimes not, by both producers and wine writers. Unsavory hustlers may ask for cash before delivery, take your money, and never deliver. The best defense against such a disaster is to deal with a reputable merchant. This is a business for the trade or high end collectors with a long relationship with a top end wine merchant. Again, caveat emptor!

For the Love of Labels

Now that you know where and when to shop for your wines, you're ready to look at the fine print. The fine print on wine labels can seem like a foreign language. But if you know how to decode a label, it's like having a secret, almost mystical knowledge. Even if you read no further, the following information is guaranteed to increase your wine IQ and EQ (enjoyment quotient!).

Vintages and Vino

Since 99 percent of all the wines produced are meant to be consumed young (i.e., within the first five years), you really don't have to worry about the vintage you are buying when you purchase an everyday wine. All you want is a wine that is young (i.e., a recent vintage) and in good condition. If you are shopping for California wines, vintage hardly matters at all. The weather is so consistent that vintage variations of quality are quite minimal. Buying wines from the Old

World (including France, Italy, and Spain) requires some knowledge of the good years from the bad, but here is a tip that doesn't require a chart: Look at the same wine with two different vintages. The price differential will tell you which vintage in that region is rated more highly.

My shopping advice on vintages is: In the great years, buy the lesser label; in the lesser years, buy the great label. Why? In the great vintage years everyone makes very good wine and therefore there is no need to pay the premium for the big names. The 2000 red Bordeaux are a good example. You couldn't go wrong even buying wines from producers with lesser reputations. On the other hand, in poor vintages only the top brands make outstanding wine.

However, if you are making a serious investment in a special occasion wine or buying by the case, you should take the time to talk to your friendly wine merchant. If you express an interest, you'll more likely be steered to the better years. I rely on Sherry-Lehmann's Joe Uris, who knows the good and great vintages and can draw from their staggeringly large inventory of everyday, fine, and rare bottles from wine-growing regions all over the world.

To Filter or Not to Filter

Some wines feature "unfiltered" on their labels when most don't even mention it. What does it mean, and should you care?

Most Americans think a wine should be perfectly clear and would be very leery about drinking a red wine if it was hazy or there was sediment in the glass. So wines made in commercial quantities, for immediate consumption, are filtered.

The word "unfiltered" on a red wine label usually indicates a wine with some residual sediment in the bottle. Many wine producers who make fine wines intended for long-term aging promote the fact that they don't filter their wines. They believe, as I do, that these extra particles of flavor should not be swept away by filtering prior to bottling. I equate filtering to making the gravy at Thanksgiving. I would never scrape away all the crusty particles in the pan where the turkey was roasted because when these particles are left with the drippings . . . the resulting gravy has much more flavor!

On French wine you will see the words *non filtre*. A bottle from Australia or California would say "unfiltered." So start checking wine labels for these terms if you love rich gravy and believe in these flavor particles.

Some white wines also have a kind of sediment, called tartrates, that look like salt crystals in your wineglass. They are a by-product of really cold fermentation and you shouldn't give a toss about them—these crystals are harmless, tasteless, and to be ignored.

The Value of Labels

Vieilles vignes means "old vines" in French. The belief that older vines make better wine is much used in marketing European wines and has more recently been adopted in California and the Barossa Valley in Australia. As vines age, they produce less fruit, so the remaining fruit has less competition for sunlight and nutrients. They produce grapes, and therefore wine, with more concentrated flavors. Old World, European *vieilles vignes* are thirty-five to fifty years old. Some vines may be older. With grafting of new vines onto old root stock, the age of the resulting vine may be impossible to tell. In the New World wines, *vieilles vignes* means only fifteen to twenty years old. So *vieilles vignes* or "vv" on a French wine label, or "old vines" on an Australian or California wine label, is like finding a free prize in the cereal box.

Meritage

Meritage (rhymes with heritage) is not a varietal wine (made from only one specific variety of grape) or the name of a particular wine, nor is it short for merit badge. It is a California wine blended in a style similar to the great Bordeaux wines of France, which contain primarily Cabernet Sauvignon, Merlot, and Cabernet Franc grapes. For most of California's winemaking history, blended wines were considered inferior to straight varietals. But the finest French Bordeaux wines are blends, and the California wine producers decided they needed to create a term for this new style of blended wine that would liberate it from the poor reputation of past blends. So they held a contest for what to call these wines. The name chosen was "meritage," which sounds sort of French and could be a blend of "merit" and "heritage." It could also suggest the idea of a marriage between several grape varieties. In drinking these wines, you taste the full range of the creativity of the winemaker freed of the restrictions of varietal labeling that requires 75 percent of the wine come from one grape variety. Thus the winemaker has the opportunity to create exciting blends that could end up as legendary wines. Accordingly, a meritage wine is like a signature dish at a restaurant where the chef has free rein to combine whatever ingredients he or she chooses. While I certainly enjoy my fair share of Cabernet, I prefer this style of blended wine with its more complex and interesting flavors . . . sort of the same way I love a good hamburger, but prefer a hamburger with "the works." If you are at the wine store or a restaurant and want to try a meritage but can't remember this term, no problem: Just ask the salesperson or the sommelier to recommend a California Bordeaux blend. Here's a list of recent vintage meritage wines to fit every budget:

**MERITAGE WINES
(A.K.A. BORDEAUX BLENDS)**

2003 Claret from Francis Ford Coppola Diamond Collection, $17

NV* Cain Cuvée from Cain Vineyard, $26 (the second label** of Cain Five, $100)

2003 Decoy Napa Valley Red Wine, $28

2002 Ciff Lede Vineyards Claret, $32

2002 Estancia Red Meritage from Estancia, $35

2001 Vintage Reserve from Firestone, $35

2002 Magnificat from Franciscan, $40

NV* Overture from Opus One, $45 (the second label** of Opus One, $165)

2002 Tapestry Reserve from Beaulieu Vineyard, $50

2003 Trilogy from Flora Springs, $60

2002 Cinq Cepages from Chateau St Jean, $75

2002 Cain Five from Cain Vineyards, $100

2001 Rubicon from Rubicon Estate, $110

2003 Jason Red from Pahlmeyer, $55 (the second label** of Pahlmeyer Proprietary Red, $110)

2002 Pahlmeyer Proprietary Red, $110

2002 Arietta Proprietary Red "H Block," $125

2002 Insignia from Joseph Phelps, $150

2002 Opus One from Mondavi, $165

> **NV, non-vintage, means the grapes that went into making these red wines aren't from one harvest year but are a blend of several years. Champagne can also be called "NV" for the same reason.*

> ***You see some wineries listed above have "second" labels. See page 102 to find out why these are such great bargains.*

"Name" Brands

You are faced with several bottles of the same wine made by different wine producers. Which should you pick? The answer may be right on the label. A small number of specialty importers use the names of the experts who selected their wines. These experts seek out and choose those that are the most interesting and best value (not necessarily the cheapest). The experts' names will usually appear on the label: "A Robert Haas Selection."

Add the names of these six wine selectors to the list of wines you want to try, and take the list with you to the store: Kermit Lynch and Robert Kacher for all French wines, Louis Dressner for Loire Valley wines, Robert Haas for Burgundies, Leonardo Locascio for wines from Italy, and Michael Skurnik importing from around the world.

Decoding Champagne Labels

Suppose you want to buy a good bottle of non-vintage Champagne in the $25 to $35 price range. You see a well-known brand, but there are lots of unfamiliar names on the shelf. Are they as good? If you are in a store with options other than the best known brands, chances are that there is sales staff with some helpful wine savvy. They may—or may not—know the following tip:

At the bottom edge of every Champagne label two tiny letters appear preceding a six-digit license number. Two of these abbreviations, "NM" and "RM," are good clues as to what's inside those seductive-looking bottles.

Almost all mass-market Champagnes are NM wines, *negociant-manipulants*. These are the large companies that buy grapes in addition to their vineyard holdings, then blend and produce very large quantities of Champagne. The quality of NM wines runs the gamut from okay to superb.

RM means *recoltant-manipulant,* a small grower and producer who makes, bottles, and sells Champagne, usually from grapes grown in his own vineyards. Many *recoltants-manipulants* own vineyards designated Grand Cru—the best quality. This is the Champagne equivalent of estate bottled. Most RMs are attractively priced and are really worth seeking out since the quality is usually good to superb. If you find one of these Champagnes, you can add them to your show-off choices listed on page 159.

The Paper Chase

 Wine bottles have not always sported those eye-catching paper labels we admire today. Historically, wine stored in cellars wasn't labeled as it could be identified by its bin number or the stamp on the bottle shoulder. Wines were also etched with the name of the buyer (T. Jefferson, for example), the name of the vintage, 1784, and the wine, Château Lafite. But when storage came "above ground" and it was necessary to identify the name of the wine, tags made of wood, bone, or ivory were initially used. They gradually gave way to the paper labels we know today.

Food
and *Wine*

Y ou've come home from an exhausting day at
the office, and while you really would like
to cook, you just can't manage it. You've barely
kicked your shoes off and you're already looking
at the local Chinese restaurant's takeout menu.
You choose an egg roll, an order of spicy, salty
Szechuan chicken, and some dry-roasted green
beans in black bean sauce. While you're waiting
for your dinner to arrive, you open up a chilled
bottle of inexpensive Alsatian Riesling that you
picked up on a whim. A few minutes later, you're
sitting in front of the television in your
sweatpants, eating dinner directly out of the white
cardboard delivery cartons, with wooden
chopsticks. You absentmindedly take a sip of the
Riesling, and suddenly you stop. You take another
sip of wine, and another bite of the chicken. You
examine the bottle to make sure that this was the
inexpensive stuff the guy at the wine store
recommended because it tastes so stupendous. Its
perfectly soft, round fruitiness cuts through the
salty, spicy edge of the Chinese food, and as if by
magic, this $20 dinner (which you're enjoying
while wearing your favorite fuzzy slippers) is one
of the most delicious you've had in a long while,

and the $11.99 Alsatian Riesling the wine clerk urged you to try tastes like a million bucks.

Was it the food? Or was it the wine? Uniting food with wine is less dramatic than choosing a life partner, but fighting should not be permitted at the table! The basic guidelines of matching are simple enough that, once you understand them, your dining experiences will be forever changed . . . for the better. No more clashing flavors! No more bickering bottles! No more angst over what goes with what!

In this chapter I'll tell you exactly how to pair wines and foods in a way that will enrich your daily life and make you the toast of the town when it comes to entertaining.

A great and expensive wine can be bland, boring, or bitter if the wrong food is served along with it. By the same token, an inexpensive, lower-tier wine can be an absolute show-stopper if you pick just the right menu. How to choose the perfect wine to match the food you're eating? It involves neither luck, nor money, nor advanced wine education.

Despite what some so-called wine connoisseurs and "taste technicians" might lead you to believe, there really *are* no hard and fast rules when it comes to pairing wine with food. But there are personal preferences. You may always *prefer* a light, crisp Sauvignon Blanc to a full-bodied Chardonnay. But, in the same way that you'd never wear a pair of hiking boots with a tuxedo, the fact is that not all wines go well with all foods. If you match your favorite full-bodied red to, say, a nice piece of Texas-style barbecued brisket, that heavy-bodied wine will suddenly blossom, as if by a miracle. The barbecue will taste better than it ever has in your recollection, and so will your favorite Zinfandel. But match the same juicy, flavor-packed dish with a light-bodied red wine, and that wine will simply disappear under the weight and spice in the meat.

The right wine makes good food great and great food fabulous, and vice versa.

A Few Simple Rules for Mating Your Wine

If you're just beginning to experiment with food and wine pairing, you need to know a little, but not too much—like using your cell phone for simply making calls—or you may suffer from overload. Here are some simple guidelines that are easy to remember, logical, and even intuitive. Think of them as your default wine knowledge setting.

1. **The Weighting Game.** Match the weight of the food to the weight of the wine. A heavy, full-bodied wine can turn into a wine "bully" if you try to drink it with a light little piece of grilled fish. So, if you're having steamed scallops, enjoy them with a wine that is light and crisp. Likewise, if the food that you're eating is heavy and flavorful, match it to a wine that is heavy enough to stand up to its power.

2. **Play the Numbers.** No doubt you've been diligently reading the tiny print on labels to find out how many grams of cholesterol or carbohydrates your food contains. Why not

make it a habit to read your wine labels? The quickest, most foolproof way to figure out any wine's weight is to read the label. Somewhere, in tiny print, you'll find the percentage of alcohol contained in the wine. This number is the key to unlocking how light or heavy the wine will taste. A light- to medium-bodied wine is between 11 and 13.0 percent, while a big wine is 13.5 percent all the way up to a clobbering 15.5 percent.

3. **Build Bridges.** Bridge wines are medium-bodied enough to span the gap between light and heavy foods. When people at the table are ordering fish, chicken, and meat, and you only want to order one bottle of wine that would be delicious with everything, a bridge wine comes to the rescue. It should span the gap between light- and heavy-weight dishes. Two of my standbys are Pinot Noir (from any region) and Australian Shiraz. You can count on these wines like two old friends who are supportive and forgiving no matter what state you're in.

I'll go into more detail on all three of these subjects later in the chapter. But if you were to read no further, chances are good you would fare fairly well in your wine mating game.

White Cuffs

The next level of your wine knowledge setting is more advanced, like learning how to use your cell phone to text message or go on the Internet. I call it **WHITE CUFFS.** This easy and elegant acronym will enable you to make the right wine selection whether you are in a three-star restaurant in Paris, a local Italian trattoria in Peoria, or the wine shop around the corner. **WHITE CUFFS** stands for the six most important components that go into your wine selection:

WEIGHT (The W reminds you of White)
COOKING METHOD
UMAMI
FAT IN THE MEAT
FATTY INGREDIENTS
SPICY, SALTY, OR SMOKY

If you can remember **WHITE CUFFS**, your selection process will be simplified, and will allow you to choose wisely. (See pages 150–151 for examples.) To make things even easier, simply refer to my master **WHITE CUFFS** chart, on pages 50–55. Clip it out, carry it with you, tack it to your refrigerator, keep a copy of it in your purse or in your glove compartment, and you'll be prepared for any wine pairing occasion.

WEIGHT

Throw caution to the wind and be color-blind: Consider weight *before* you even think white or red. I know this sounds like wine heresy, but trust the Wine Diva. It works. The first element of **WHITE CUFFS** is also the most elementary. Considering the relative weight of your potential food and wine choices is rather like sizing someone up for a first date: You're not going to be able to assess a person's subtle characteristics, but you do get a general overall impression just by looking. You can start with either what food you feel like having or which wine you feel like drinking.

The Weight of Food

In terms of food, weight often does correspond to its actual weight in ounces: A serving of filet of sole weighs less than one of filet mignon.

Light	Caesar salad
	Mesclun salad with goat cheese
	Salad Nicoise
Weight of food?	Light, so wine should be light-bodied.
Cooking method?	Uncooked foods like salad work best with unoaked white wines such as Sauvignon Blanc, Pinot Grigio, Riesling, Muscadet, and Chablis. If you prefer red, opt for lightly-oaked reds like Pinot Noir, Chianti, Valpolicella, and Bardolino.
Umami in dish?	No
Fat in meat/fish?	No
Fatty ingredients?	No
S Factor?	Yes. Anchovies, cheese, olives, and capers are salty. Lots of tannin in a wine and salty ingredients don't go well together, so avoid oaky Chardonnay and tannic Cabernet. This is the same advice echoed above due to cooking method.

Light	Crab meat with tartar or remoulade sauce
	Shrimp cocktail
	Raw oysters
	Crabmeat salad with Louis dressing
	Eggs Benedict with Hollandaise sauce
	Mushroom omelets
	Tuna or salmon tartare
Weight of food?	Light, so wine should be light-bodied.
Cooking method?	Raw foods and those boiled in water work best with unoaked white wines like Pinot Grigio, Sancerre, Sauvignon Blanc, and Muscadet. If you prefer red, opt for subtly-oaked reds like Beaujolais-Villages, Bourgeuil, and Chinon.
Umami in dish?	Not in eggs, tuna, salmon, but it's present in shellfish (shrimp, oysters, and crab) and mushrooms. Foods with umami need wines with little or no tannin, which translates to little or no oak. This is the same advice echoed above due to cooking method.
Fatty ingredients?	Hollandaise, tartar, remoulade, and Louis sauce are thick and creamy and so have an affinity for buttery California Chardonnays. Although crisp, unoaked whites seem like the perfect pairing with the main ingredient, you could opt for an oaky Chardonnay with the eggs Benedict, crab cakes, and the crabmeat salad because of their sauces.
Fat in meat/fish?	No
S Factor?	No

Light

	BBQ shrimp with ginger, lime, and cilantro Spicy sautéed crab cakes
Weight of food?	Light, so wine should be light-bodied.
Cooking method?	BBQ and sautéing turn the food brown, which means serving oaked wines.
Umami in dish?	Yes, in shellfish. Foods with umami pair best with wines that have no/low tannin, which translates to no oak/light oak flavors. So choose more subtly oaked French Chardonnays from Burgundy or the lightly oaked or "naked" Chardonnays described on page 148. If you prefer red, pick lightly to moderately oaked reds such as Barbera and Dolcetto from Italy and Merlot from Chile or Italy.
Fat in meat/fish?	No
Fatty ingredients?	No
S Factor?	Yes, which means steer clear of tannic wines like Cabernet and heavily oaked Chardonnay. This is the same advice echoed above due to presence of umami.

Light

	Fried shrimp with cocktail sauce Fried calamari with marinara dipping sauce
Weight of food?	Light, so wine should be light-bodied.
Cooking method?	Frying in oil means you should use an unoaked white wine like a Pinot Grigio, Sauvignon Blanc, or a non-vintage Champagne or bubbly, which cuts through the oil.
Umami in dish?	Yes, in tomatoes and shrimp. So steer clear of tannic wines and reach for no tannin, unoaked whites like those mentioned above, or be color-blind and opt for low tannin reds like Pinot Noir and Beaujolais-Villages.
Fat in meat/fish?	No
Fatty ingredients?	No
S Factor?	Cocktail sauce and marinara sauce can be spicy, so avoid tannic wines like Cabernet and heavily oaked Chardonnay. This is the same advice echoed above due to presence of umami.

Medium	Veal picata with lemon and capers
	Ham
	Chicken cordon bleu
	Fettuccine with sun-dried tomatoes, olives, and prosciutto
	Spaghetti carbonara with Parmesan and pancetta
	Fusilli pasta with pesto sauce
Weight of food?	Medium, so wine should be medium-bodied.
Cooking method?	Baking, sautéing turns veal, ham, or chicken brown, which means an oaked wine. Although pasta is cooked in water, which would normally call for an unoaked wine, pasta is the accompaniment to the sauce, which has the starring role. So look at the ingredients in the sauce to point you to an ideal wine match.
Umami present?	No
Fatty meat/fish?	No
Fatty ingredients?	No
S Factor?	Yes. Each dish has prominent salty ingredients (capers, ham, cheese, sun-dried tomatoes, olives, prosciutto, pancetta, and pesto sauce) so avoid tannic Cabernet and heavily oaked Chardonnays and opt for less tannic (subtly oaked) whites like Burgundy, Bordeaux, and lightly oaked and "naked" Chardonnays (page 148). If you prefer red wine, pick medium-bodied, less tannic reds, including Rioja Crianza, Côtes du Rhône, Barbera, and Chianti Classico. S Factor foods also pair well with no tannin, unoaked white wines. So think of medium-bodied Pinot Gris, Albariño, Rueda, and Grüner Veltliner as alternatives.

Medium	Paella with spicy sausage
	Beef tacos or enchiladas with jalapeño chilies
	Chicken curry
	Ahi Tuna with ginger, garlic, and mint
	Thai-style pork tenderloin
	Swordfish with cilantro, cumin, and lime salsa
	Smoked duck breast with orange sauce
Weight of food?	Medium, so wine should be medium-bodied.
Cooking method?	Baking, sautéing, grilling; baking turns ingredients brown, which means use an oaked wine.
Umami present?	No
Fatty meat/fish?	No
Fatty ingredients?	No

S Factor?	Yes. Each dish has either spicy or smoky ingredients so avoid tannic Cabernet and heavily oaked Chardonnays and opt for less tannic wines whose acidity and sweetness stand up to the spicy/salty/smoky flavors. Reds include Beaujolais Cru, Merlot, Shiraz, and red Burgundy. Whites include white Burgundy and white Bordeaux and lightly oaked Chardonnays on page 148.

Medium	Lobster with butter Thai-style sea bass in a lemongrass, coconut cream sauce Sole meuniere Scallops in a cream sauce
Weight of food?	Medium, so wine should be medium-bodied.
Cooking method?	Broiling, sautéing, and grilling turns fish and seafood brown, which means an oaked wine.
Umami present?	No
Fatty meat/fish?	No
Fatty ingredients?	Yes. Butter, cream, and sour cream are the perfect dates for those oaky, buttery, creamy California Chardonnays.
S Factor?	No

Medium	Spaghetti Bolognese with tomato basil sauce Chicken cacciatore Veal parmigiana Pizza with sausage Wild mushroom risotto
Weight of food?	Medium, so wine should be medium-bodied.
Cooking method?	Baking, sautéing, and grilling turns meat/chicken/veal brown, which means an oaked wine.
Umami present?	Yes, in tomatoes and mushrooms. Get in gear with less tannic reds like Barbera, Tuscan reds like Chianti, Montepulciano and Vino Nobile, Pinot Noir, Merlot, and Shiraz. If you are in a mood for white wine, pour a lightly oaked or "naked" Chardonnay or opt for some of Italy's great whites like Fiano, Greco, or Arneis.
Fatty meat/fish?	No
Fatty ingredients?	No
S Factor?	No

Heavy	Filet mignon London broil Flank steak Ostrich
Weight of food?	Heavy, so wine should be full-bodied.
Cooking method?	Baking, pan frying, and grilling turns meat brown, so use an oaked wine.
Umami present?	No
Fatty meat/fish?	No. These lean cuts have precious little fat that can act as a buffer against astringent tannins of a big Cabernet. So opt for a less tannic wine. Since these meats lack the rich flavor that comes from lots of fat, drink wines that are fruity to counter balance the blander meat. Luckily there are many wines that have moderate tannin and are fruit forward. Reds include Pinot Noir, Shiraz, and Merlot. If you get red wine headaches and need a full-bodied white with only moderate tannin, try a white Burgundy, white Bordeaux, or lightly oaked Chardonnay.
Fatty ingredients?	No
S Factor?	No

Heavy	Porterhouse/rib eye/sirloin steak Prime rib roast Meatloaf Hamburger Veal and lamb chops or roast
Weight of food?	Heavy, so wine should be full-bodied.
Cooking method?	Roasting and grilling turns meat brown, so choose an oaked wine.
Umami present?	No
Fatty meat/fish?	Yes. Fat coats the palate and acts as a buffer against the high level of tannin in Cabernet, red Bordeaux, Syrah, Malbec, Chateauneuf-du-Pape, Barolo, and Brunello d'Montalcino. If you get red wine headaches and need a full-bodied white with only moderate tannin, try a white Burgundy, white Bordeaux, or lightly oaked Chardonnay.
Fatty ingredients?	No
S Factor?	No

Heavy	Chile con carne Steak Diane BBQ spare ribs
Weight of food?	Heavy, so wine should be full-bodied.
Cooking method?	Browned meat calls for an oaked wine.
Umami present?	No
Fatty meat/fish?	Yes. These dishes might seem ideal for serving Cabernet, but when you consider the S Factor below, it changes the picture completely.
Fatty ingredients?	No
S Factor?	Yes. Spices in the chili, black pepper in the steak sauce, and fiery BBQ sauce cry out for a fruity wine to dampen the heat of these prominent spicy ingredients. Cabernet is not a fruity wine, so turn instead to Pinot Noir, Shiraz, Merlot, or Zinfandel. Moreover, S Factor foods don't partner well with tannic wines.

Heavy	Brisket Pot roast Osso bucco
Weight of food?	Heavy, so wine should be full-bodied.
Cooking method?	Slow cooking turns meat brown, which means an oaked wine.
Umami present?	Umami is present in slow cooked meats so avoid tannic reds like Cabernet, Syrah, and Malbec as well as oaky Chardonnay. Instead pair foods containing umami with wines that are less tannic like Pinot Noir, Barbera, Merlot, and Shiraz. Less tannic whites (translation: less oaky) are white Burgundy and white Bordeaux and subtly-oaked Chardonnays listed on page 148.
Fatty meat/fish?	No. Pot roast and veal shanks are lean meats, which need fruitier wines like Pinot Noir, Barbera, Merlot, and Shiraz or lightly oaked Chardonnay (which lets the fruit shine through). This is the same advice mentioned above due to presence of umami.
Fatty ingredients?	No
S Factor?	No

A casserole is far heavier than a salad. You can also think about what sorts of things you naturally feel like eating when it's bitter cold outside versus on a sultry summer evening. The hot summer dishes are going to be light whereas we think of winter menus as heavy.

So, I'd group the most common dishes this way, from light to heavy:

— LIGHTWEIGHTS —

Calamari	Oysters
Bruschetta	Salads
Crabs	Salmon/tuna tartare
Crudités	Sashimi
Eggs Benedict	Shrimp
Gazpacho	Sole
Guacamole	Sushi
Mussels	Tabouleh
Omelettes	Vegetables

— MEDIUMWEIGHTS —

Chicken	Risotto
Duck	Salmon
Empanadas	Sea bass
Enchiladas	Steak tartare
Ham	Swordfish
Lobster	Tacos
Paella	Tuna
Pasta	Turkey
Pizza	Veal scaloppini
Pork	

— HEAVYWEIGHTS —

Chile con carne	Pot roast
Hamburgers	Steak
Lamb (roasts, chops, kebobs)	Veal chops
Meatloaf	Venison
Osso bucco	Wild boar

The Weight of Wine

When it comes to deciphering how light- or full-bodied a wine will taste, there's no substitute for knowing its alcohol content. The lower the percentage, the lighter the wine will seem when you drink it. Alcohol content trumps color in the weighting game. Try this little experiment to prove it to yourself in a most delightful way: Taste a white wine like a California Chardonnay with an alcohol level of 14 percent or higher and compare it to an 11.5 to 12.5 percent red. Here are some French reds to experiment with: a red Burgundy (made from Pinot Noir), Chinon, and Bourgeuil (made from Cabernet Franc), and Beaujolais-Villages (made from Gamay). Which one is "lighter"? I bet you'll find the lower-alcohol reds seem lighter. So go ahead and enjoy that "light" red instead of the usual white with your salmon, tuna, and bass!

Even within types of wines, the alcohol content varies tremendously. So, for example, Chardonnay may come in a truly light Chablis at 12 percent, a Meursault at 13 percent, or a California Chardonnay at a heavyweight champion percentage of 14.5. If you're having shrimp, the Chablis will go quite nicely, but the California wine will overpower the poor little crustacean. Learn to read the wine label for the alcohol content the way you read cans and packages of food for carbohydrates or sodium. Eleven percent (or less) to 13 percent alcohol wines are light- to medium-bodied and go with similar weight dishes, while 13.5 to 15.5 percent are full-bodied wines that go best with heavier fare.

If you're serving lightweight foods, go for a light-bodied wine and be color-blind. Good, no-fail picks for

the Weight of Wines

WHITES

Light-bodied (Unoaked No tannin)	Medium-bodied (Unoaked No tannin)	Full-bodied (Oaked Moderate tannin)
	NEW WORLD*	
Sauvignon Blanc	Chardonnay**	Chardonnay**
Sparkling***	Pinot Gris	Semillon/Chardonnay blend
	Chenin Blanc	Viognier
	Gewürztztraminer	
	Sparkling***	
	OLD WORLD	
	ITALY	
Pinot Grigio	Gavi	
Soave	Vernaccia	
Orvieto	Arneis	
Vermentino	Greco	
Prosecco (sparkling)	Fiano	
Verdicchio	Falanghina	
	SPAIN	
Cava (sparkling)	Rueda	
	Albariño	
	GERMANY	
Riesling		
Sekt (sparkling)		
	AUSTRIA	
	Grüner Veltliner	

*New World = USA, Australia, New Zealand, Chile, Argentina, and South Africa

**Can range from medium-bodied to full-bodied.

***Can range from light-bodied to medium-bodied.

REDS

Light-bodied (Little oak Low tannin)	Medium-bodied (Moderate oak Moderate tannin)	Full-bodied (Oaky More tannin)
	NEW WORLD*	
	Cabernet**	Cabernet**
	Shiraz**	Syrah**
	Merlot**	Merlot**
	Pinot Noir	"Meritage"/Bordeaux
	Barbera	Zinfandel
	Sangiovese	Malbec
	Rhône style blends	
	OLD WORLD	
	ITALY	
Bardolino	Vino Nobile di Montepulciano	Barolo
Valpolicella	Montepulciano d'Abruzzo	Barbaresco
Chianti	Chianti Classico and	Brunello di Montalcino
Barbera**	Chianti Classico Riserva	Taurasi
	Rosso di Montalcino	Super Tuscan wines
	Dolcetto	Amarone
	SPAIN	
Rioja-Crianza	Rioja Riserva	Ribera del Duero
	Rioja Gran Riserva	region wines
		Priorato region wines

Light-bodied (Unoaked No tannin)	Medium-bodied (Unoaked No tannin)	Full-bodied (Oaked Moderate tannin)
	FRANCE -Burgundy	
Chablis	Chablis Premier and Grand Cru	Corton-Charlemagne
	Most white Burgundies, e.g. Meursault	Meursault
	Pouilly-Fuissé	Puligny-Montrachet and
	St-Aubin	Chassagne-Montrachet
	St-Veran	
	St-Romain	
	Auxey-Duresses	
	Macon-Villages	
	FRANCE -Champagne	
Non-vintage	NV and Vintage	
	FRANCE -Loire Valley	
Muscadet	Pouilly-Fumé	
Cremant d'Loire	Sancerre	
(sparkling)	Vouvray	
	FRANCE -Alsace	
Pinot Blanc	Pinot Gris	
Riesling	Gewürztraminer	
	FRANCE -Rhône	
		NORTH
		white Rhône blend
		SOUTH
		white Châteauneuf-du-Pape
	FRANCE -Bordeaux	
		white Bordeaux

	REDS	
Light-bodied (Little oak Low tannin)	**Medium-bodied** (Moderate oak Moderate tannin)	**Full-bodied** (Oaky More tannin)
	FRANCE -Burgundy	
Beaujolais	Cru Beaujolais	
Beaujolais-Villages	Gevrey-Chambertin	
Burgundy (Village)	Chambolle-Musigny	
	Chorey-les-Beaune	
	Savigny-les-Beaune	
	Santennay	
	Marsannay	
	Givry	
	Mercurey	
	FRANCE -Champagne	
	FRANCE -Loire Valley	
Samur-Champigny		
Bourgeuil		
Chinon		
	FRANCE -Alsace	
	FRANCE -Rhône	
	NORTH	NORTH
	Cornas	Côte Rotie
	St-Joseph	Hermitage
	Crozes-Hermitage	
	SOUTH	SOUTH
	Côtes du Rhône	Châteauneuf-du-Pape
	FRANCE -Bordeaux	
	247 Cru Bourgeois wines	61 Great Château wines

whites are: Pinot Grigio, Frascati, Orvieto, Verdicchio, and Soave from Italy; Riesling from Alsace, Germany, Italy, and Australia; non-vintage Champagne, Pinot Blanc, Chablis, and Muscadet from France, plus ubiquitous Sauvignon Blanc. Surefire picks for lighter reds are: Beaujolais, Beaujolais-Villages, Chinon, Saumur-Champigny, and St. Nicholas de Bourgeuil from France; Chianti, Bardolino, and Valpolicella from Italy; and Rioja-Crianza from Spain.

Wines to go with medium-weight foods are a bit trickier. Chardonnay, Syrah, Shiraz, Cabernet, red Bordeaux, Merlot, Zinfandel, Champagne, and sparkling wines can be medium- or full-bodied. (Ask the wine store salesperson or the sommelier which wines are which. They know.) However, there are white and red wines that fit neatly into the medium slot. White Bordeaux (made from a blend of Sauvignon Blanc and Semillon), Spain's great Albariño, as well as Pinot Gris from Alsace and Oregon are terrific candidates that don't straddle the fence. For reds, you can't go wrong with Rioja Riserva and Gran Riserva, Chianti Classico Riserva, Côtes du Rhône, and my two favorites: Pinot Noir and Barbera di Alba.

Full-bodied wines in the red arena are Cabernet Sauvignon, red Bordeaux, Zinfandel, Syrah,

The Charm of Chardonnay

There's a sweet secret reason why we Americans adore Chardonnay. We've become almost addicted to soda and other highly sweetened drinks. Alcohol content in wine translates to a sweet taste in the mouth. Guess what a typical percentage of alcohol in California Chardonnay is? It's 14 percent or higher, enough to satisfy our collective sweet tooth.

Shiraz, and Merlot, as well as Italy's triple crown winners Barolo, Barbaresco, Brunello de Montalcino, and the French Rhônes, Chateauneuf-du-Pape, Cote Rôtie, and Hermitage. In order to stay color-blind, there are hefty whites that could step in such as California and Australian Chardonnay, Chardonnay/Semillon blends from Australia, French and California Viognier, Alsatian Gewurztraminer, and vintage Champagne.

Cooking Method

Is your humble piece of chicken coming to you deep-fried? Lightly fried with a squeeze of lemon? Sautéed in butter? Sautéed in olive oil? Stir-fried? Plain broiled? Most of us, when we're pairing wine with our food, never really stop to consider the fact that different cooking methods applied to the same food chemically alter that food. You don't need to know the scientific details because you can actually see the effects with the naked eye: Heat and fat applied in a direct and consistent manner result in caramelization, that beautiful brown with a sweet, nutty flavor. Poaching or boiling in clear liquids such as water doesn't affect the original flavor of a main ingredient nearly as much.

Imagine the difference in taste between a poached filet of sole and sole sautéed in butter. Or the difference between steak tartare (which is uncooked), steak au poivre (which is pan-grilled), and beef stew (which is braised). When you boil, steam, or poach anything, you are adding no flavor—or color—to the dish. But when you sauté, braise, or roast, you are physically browning the meat, which in a process that *adds* sweetness—and color.

Virtually all red wines and some white wines develop much of their specific flavors because they pick up the subtleties of aroma and flavor from the different kinds of barrels they are aged in (usually American or French oak); these flavors are generally described as "vanilla," "toasty," "coconut," and "smoky"—and all are arguably variations of "sweetness."

Therefore, chicken that has been sautéed in butter is more delicious when paired with a buttery, flavorful, oaked wine, whereas a lightly poached piece of chicken will do better when paired with a light and crisply juicy, unoaked wine. Likewise, fried foods (tempura, fritto misto, fried shrimp, wiener schnitzel) can run the gamut from light to heavy, and are often accompanied by a squirt of lemon; but they all fare well when paired with a crisp, light, unoaked white wine.

I like to help people think about cooking method by invoking color. Food cooked in water, which is clear, calls for a clear wine. So for poached, steamed, or boiled food, serve a clear white unoaked wine. This principle can extend to raw foods such as oysters, salad, or vegetables that you clean in water. And let's not forget food fried in clear-colored oil. Stir-fried and deep fried foods also go best with unoaked wines.

Food that turns brown, or caramelized, by sautéing in butter, roasting, or grilling fairly sings when paired with oaked wine. After all, oak is a wood, and wood is brown, so remember brown (browned food) equals wood (oaked wine).

Of Oak and Chardonnay

Wines made from the Chardonnay grape are the most popular white wines in the United States. If made in America, these wines are called Chardonnay, after the varietal. In France, wines are named after the place where the Chardonnay grapes are grown—for example, Burgundy or the village of St. Aubin. One big difference between Chardonnays from the U.S. and France is oak flavor. The amount of oakiness is controlled by the winemaker, not by nature. Oak flavor is added to

The Color of Wine

 We have talked a lot about oaked and unoaked pairings. At this point you may be asking yourself: Is there a way to tell wines apart before bringing the glass to your lips? YES—on sight, in fact. You may have wanted to order an unoaked white because you remembered certain WHITE CUFFS guidelines, but the glass of the wine you ordered is set before you and it is a bright yellow or golden color. While you can't change the wine, you can experiment, knowing in advance just by looking at the color of the wine in the glass that it's not "supposed to be" a great match and learn from the experience.

How can you tell the difference between the oaked and unoaked wines?

WHITE

Oak = color of the wine (straw yellow, yellow, yellow/gold, gold, yellow/brown)
Unoaked = absence of color in the wine (clear, pale yellow/green, palest yellow)

The colors for oaked wines that can age (white Burgundy, Chardonnay, and white Bordeaux) have been listed above from youthful to mature.

RED

You can't tell by sight if a red wine is oaked or unoaked. But since virtually all reds see some oak (except Beaujolais Nouveau), color is not a factor. The amount of oakiness (vanilla, butterscotch, smokiness, coconut flavors, etc.) is detected purely by smell and taste.

Similarly, you can tell the body of a wine on sight. Pour yourself a glass of Pinot Noir and Cabernet. Stand up and look into the wines. Or stay seated and hold them up to the light. The lighter colored red wine (shades of ruby, garnet) will be the medium body Pinot Noir and the deeper colored red wine (purple, brick red, red brown) will be the Cabernet/red Bordeaux. Color also corresponds to the level of refreshing acidity in a red wine with the medium bodied, lighter reds having a more refreshing quality and deeper, fuller bodied reds having just moderate acidity.

As Cabernet/red Bordeaux matures note that the color will lessen and go from purple, brick red to red/brown. However, as youngsters, Barolo, Barbaresco, and Brunello never start out deep purple, but lessen in color from brick red to red/brown.

wines by fermenting the wine in oak barrels in which the young wine absorbs the oak flavor. Additional oak flavor may be imparted by aging the wines in oak barrels or adding oak chips in the tank.

I have used the terms *oaked* or *unoaked*, but in truth three styles exist—heavily oaked, lightly oaked, and non-oaked, sometimes called naked Chardonnay. American producers are making all three styles. Although your preference among these variations is entirely personal, the presence or absence of oak does affect the food and wine equation.

So consider the cooking method of the food you are going to enjoy *before* you decide what wine to order in the restaurant, or which wine to buy at the store:

- When boiling, steaming, or poaching food, eating raw foods and fried foods, select either an unoaked white, sparkling wine, or non-vintage Champagne that is crisp, and light to medium-bodied. Still whites include Pinot Grigio, Sauvignon Blanc, Sancerre, and Muscadet.

- When sautéing, roasting, baking, grilling, or barbecuing, select a medium- to full-bodied oaky red or white wine. Whites include Chardonnay and white Burgundy, and reds include Pinot Noir, Merlot, Shiraz, Cabernet, and Zinfandel.

Umami

Once you understand the issues of weight, cooking method, and ingredients, it's time to move on to another unique taste twist, one that may be new to you but which Asian gourmets have been talking about for more than a thousand years. Difficult to translate from the Japanese, umami (ooh-MAH-me) is referred to as the "fifth taste," the other four being salty, bitter, sweet, and sour. Umami is most often described as *savory*, *meaty*, and *pungent*; foods high in umami include tomatoes, shellfish (especially oysters), mushrooms (especially shiitake), truffles, Parmesan cheese, consommés, long-braised meats, soy sauce, Worcestershire sauce, and cured meats (sausages, prosciutto, guanciale, speck, bacon, any kind of American ham). Umami-infused foods can be tricky to pair with wine because umami emphasizes tannins in wine and makes them more bitter and astringent. Tannins, you say? Bear with me, and read on.

To help remember more village names in Burgundy here are two sentences:

British Petroleum votes for a member of Parliament who's into chasing S and M. Beaune, Pommard, Volnay, Meursault, Puligny-Montrachet, Chassagne-Montrachet, Santenay, and Maranges. *St. Roman's monthly auxiliary undresses at St. Aubin.* St-Romain, Monthelie, Auxey-Duresses, St-Aubin.

Ever-present in young red wines that need time to age, tannins, those astringent, pucker-worthy devils, mellow with time and take on a certain roundness and flavor interest that allows, for example, a good Bordeaux to become a mind-blowing Bordeaux over the course of fifteen years or so. That's the good news. The bad news is that when a wine is *too* tannic, the result can be disastrous for its culinary companion, not to mention your taste buds. Choose poorly, and it will feel like your gums are dried-out shoe leather and your tongue is falling off.

When you are faced with foods that are high in umami, such as oysters, braised meats, or anything in a tomato sauce, avoid tannic red wines like Cabernet and heavily oaked white wines like

Chardonnay (many are long-aged in oak barrels, which impart tannins). Instead, try the following:

Oysters: Serve crisp, unoaked white wines, like Sauvignon Blanc, Pinot Grigio, Muscadet, Sancerre. Avoid Chardonnay, White Burgundy, and Fumé Blanc (the oaked version of Sauvignon Blanc).

Braised Beef or Lamb: Serve a mature red wine—a Burgundy or an older Barolo—in which the tannins have mellowed and softened from long aging. Avoid heavily tannic reds, like Cabernet or red Bordeaux.

Anything in Tomato Sauce: Serve a lighter-weight red Italian wine, such as Dolcetto, Valpolicella, Bardolino, Barbera di Alba or Barbera di Asti, Chianti, or any Tuscan wine made from the less tannic Sangiovese grape. Again, tannic wines like Cabernet, Syrah, and Bordeaux are to be avoided.

Tannin Taming Tips

If you find yourself in a situation with an unfortunate combination of umami-filled food and tannic wine, all is not lost. I know of at least three ways to save the marriage.

The simplest way to reduce the impact of tannins in your mouth is to add fresh ground black pepper—to your food, that is, not the wine. The tannins will mellow, as if by magic.

If you're in a restaurant, ask the waiter to aerate the contents of your wine bottle in a decanter. The air mixes with the wine and softens the impression of the tannins in your mouth. If you are at home, get two glass water or orange juice pitchers, and toss the wine back and forth from one glass container to the other. Not only is this a little bit of fun, it aerates a young red wine and tames those tannins.

If you're not feeling energetic enough for the decanter method, simply swirl the wine around in your glass . . . not just to help the aromas waft up to your nose but, again, to aerate the wine and soften the tannins.

Fat in the Meat

Anyone who has followed the food world for the last twenty or so years knows that Americans are forever dieting and watching their fat intake. Despite the constant haranguing of the diet industry, more and more of us are choosing moderation over extremism. And that, of course, translates to some fat, some of the time, and less fat at other times. Naturally, some wines are better suited to foods with a higher fat content, and others to foods with a lower fat content.

It used to be a basic wine-and-food pairing rule of thumb that red meat, all of which was lumped together as "fatty," called for a big red wine. Not true. Any cut of lamb, duck, and richly marbled beef like Porterhouse, rib eye, or roast beef as well as plain old meatloaf is a wonderful match for young, tannic reds like Cabernet, Syrah, red Bordeaux, Barolo, Barbaresco, and Brunello. Why? These cuts of meat are marbled with fat, which actually coats the palate and protects our taste buds from the tannin's bitter astringency.

On the other hand, cuts of meat that are lower in fat—filet mignon or tenderloin, London broil, flank steak, hanger steak, pot roast, ostrich, for example—are best when paired with reds that have less tannin (because the meat contains comparatively less fat with which to coat and therefore protect the palate); they also generally need a fruitier wine, which balances the blander flavor of the less fatty meat. My old reliable, Pinot Noir, fits the leaner cut bill, as does Merlot.

Always pick less tannic reds when serving any kind of fish. It's a matter of chemistry: Fish takes on a metallic taste when it interacts with bitter tannin, which someone once described as tasting like "liquid aluminum foil." So again, choose Pinot Noir or Merlot to preserve the delicate deliciousness of fish.

Fatty Ingredients

Filet of sole meuniere, scallops in cream sauce, lobster with drawn butter, fettuccine Alfredo—if these are the kinds of rich, creamy, fat-filled dishes that make your heart go pitter-pat (but not stop, I hope!), then you need to have a good repertoire of wines to make your favorite foods sing.

An often overlooked part of successful wine and food pairing is paying attention to the ingredients involved in the dish that can alter your wine choice. After all, when was the last time you saw a restaurant serve a piece of plain chicken? More likely, it's something like sautéed, free-range chicken breast stuffed with aged goat cheese, prosciutto, sun-dried tomatoes, and herbs, then drenched in butter. Ingredients such as butter, cream, sour cream, and mayonnaise can alter the flavor and even the weight of the main food to such a degree that it's more important to consider them when picking a wine to go with that particular dish. Food made with fatty ingredients all go well with rich—buttery—Chardonnay. That's right, the Wine Diva actually *recommends* American

I have a bone to pick. The village of Beaune (bone) in Burgundy produces delicious, affordable reds.

Chardonnay with its high alcohol content to drink with this rich bunch of menu items. Other oaked white wines are white Burgundy (also from the Chardonnay grape), especially buttery Meursault, and white Bordeaux (a blend of Sauvignon Blanc and Semillon grapes).

However, opposites can and do attract in the world of wine, which is why high acid, unoaked whites like Sauvignon Blanc, Sancerre, Chablis, Pinot Gris, and Riesling do wonders to cut through a rich, fatty dish such as sole meuniere or scallops in a cream sauce. High acidity plays a key role in the marriage of wine and food: It creates a flavor that we often call "brightness" or "zest" or "tang" and instantly imparts a certain amount of liveliness to whatever it's paired with. It's what instinctively makes us add a squeeze of lemon to our fish or seafood.

Since you can be color-blind when selecting a wine for foods with fatty ingredients, you should be tempted to try these reds whose refreshing acidity can slice through cream, butter, sour cream, and mayonnaise: Pinot Noir, Barbera, Shiraz, Chinon, Bourgeuil, and Beaujolais Cru.

Remember, there are few, if any, hard and fast rules—except your personal preference.

The S Factor: Salty, Smoky, and Spicy

In today's culinary global village, you're bound to encounter food that's salty, smoky, spicy . . . or, as in the case of some cuisines like those of the Pacific Rim and Asia, *all three*! So, when you are standing in your local wine shop or reviewing a restaurant wine list consider the S Factor: Is what you are going to eat salty, smoky, spicy? Fatty roast lamb marries well with a big, tannic Cabernet. However, if you marinate lamb in a spicy mustard, raspberry vinegar, and rosemary sauce, the result is much different and calls for a different kind of wine, a fruity wine whose ripe fruit and sweetness can stand up to the spicy marinade. What happens when you smoke your duck, or you barbecue a piece of meat, or even add salty ingredients (capers, cheese, anchovies) to a meat dish? Those smoky and salty flavors, like the spicy mustard sauce on lamb, need sweetness as a counterweight and thus go great with what I call Pinot Noir on steroids. I'm talking about fruit

The S Factor

 S Factor wines come to the rescue and cool your palate when you are serving dishes that have spicy, salty, or smoky ingredients in them. The wines possess the following traits:

- Light- to medium-body

- Low to moderate alcohol (11 to 13 percent)

- Fruit-forward—not complex with layers of flavor

- No tannins, or low or moderate tannins

- No oak or very light oak flavors

Food-friendly S Factor wines include:

WHITES
(from light- to medium-bodied)

- Pinot Grigio
- Chablis
- Muscadet
- Pinot Blanc
- Alsatian and German Riesling

- Sauvignon Blanc
- Sancerre
- Champagne and sparkling wine

Why is Chardonnay omitted? Its higher alcohol adds heat, which should be avoided with S Factor dishes.

REDS
(from light- to full-bodied)

- Valpolicella
- Beaujolais-Villages
- Chinon and St. Nicholas de Bourgeuil (made from the Cabernet Franc grape)
- Pinot Noir
- Merlot
- Beaujolais Cru
- Shiraz/Syrah
- Zinfandel

Cabernet is not on the list because its high alcohol adds heat to foods that already have enough. Also, it's a tannic wine, making S Factor dishes taste bitter and astringent.

bombs like Shiraz and Zinfandel. In fact, one adage I've heard hits it on the head: *If you flame it, Zin can tame it!*

Salty, smoky, or spicy foods also need a firefighter to come to the rescue to dampen the heat or saltiness in the foods. It's the acidity in the wine that does this job. Just as you instinctively grab a cold beer when eating S Factor foods, try to think of wines that serve the same purpose. Most people don't think of Champagne and sparkling wine as "food" wines because they're relegated like Cinderella into a corner and stereotyped as wines only for celebrations, at a wedding, or as an aperitif. Yet Champagne and sparkling wine, with their fruity effervescence, are perfect foils for the S Factor. Those first tiny bubbles are refreshing with a prickle of CO_2 like the fizz of the soft drinks and beer we drank in our youth. Champagne and sparkling wines absolutely shine with smoky, salty, spicy foods.

If you prefer a still wine, select one that has little or no oak: Too much oak will compete with the vibrant flavors of your dish. Instead, you want wines with refreshing acidity to cut the fire in the food and enough sweetness (ripe fruit) to offset the same issue. Make sure that a white wine is light, crisply juicy, and unoaked. If red wine is what you're looking for, choose one that is low in tannins, low in oak, and medium in body.

Selections Made Simple

Go ahead and say it . . . I hear it coming. All of this information about tannins and fruit, oak and umami, and you're wondering, "Whatever happened to the days when you served white wine with fish or chicken, and red wine with meat, and that was that?"

I'll say it again. There are no absolutes—no hard and fast rules about what kind of wine should be paired with what kind of food. On the other hand, if you want to make a more sophisticated decision based on more criteria, you should begin to consider the weight, cooking method, umami, S Factor, fat in the meat, and fatty ingredients.

All of this said, there are certainly wines that can simplify the selection process. The "usual suspects" among white wines that people order most often include Pinot Grigio, Sauvignon Blanc, and Chardonnay; reds include Pinot Noir, Merlot, and Cabernet. But just as you select pocket squares to add a dash to your jacket or an unusual pin to your dress, here are some unsung heroes that will add color and flair to your wine and food pairings.

Out of the Box White Wines

Riesling (light-body)

Nothing marries better with more types and styles of food than Riesling, the Little Black Dress of the wine world (because it goes with nearly everything, on nearly every occasion). Do not confuse Riesling with the overly sweet, cloying stuff called Liebfraumilch that you may have tried years back. Fresh and bright-tasting Alsatian Riesling and German Riesling Kabinett (pronounced just like "cabinet") and Riesling that say "trocken" (meaning dry) on the front label go with virtually all seafood and vegetable dishes, as well as a host of Asian foods.

Riesling also comes in sweeter, fuller-bodied versions called "Spätlese" and "Auslese," which provide luscious counterpoints for heavy Asian spice and anything cooked in coconut milk (like Thai food), as well as sweet appetizers and meats, from glazed chicken wings to sautéed foie gras to your grandmother's holiday ham.

Pinot Blanc (light-body)

From Alsace in France, a juicy white versatile enough to be enjoyed as an aperitif before dinner, at a cocktail reception, with lunch, or with appetizers as a first course at dinner.

And let's not forget some delicious Italian light-bodied entries: Arneis (sounds like "our niece"), Greco di Tufo (Greek tough guy), Vermentino (vermin), Fiano de Avellino (which can be referred to as just Fiano—think "piano"), and Vernaccia de San Gemignano (Gemignano rhymes with piano). To remember all five you could say to yourself: "Our niece loves this Greek tough guy who's a real vermin but he plays the piano in San Gemignano." These are unoaked wines that appear on most wine lists in Italian restaurants and in wine stores everywhere.

Pinot Gris (medium-body)

Big brother of Pinot Grigio, Pinot Gris is made in Oregon, as well as Alsace in France. A medium-bodied, unoaked white that is brimming with refreshing acidity and fruit, Pinot Gris is wonderful with Asian dishes like chicken curry and chicken satay, as well as quiche lorraine, pork chops, and veal dishes.

Grüner Veltliner (medium-body)

Deliciously light and peppery, this undersung white wine from Austria is experiencing a rebirth in the United States, as well it should: Its fragrance, flavor, and modest alcohol content make it a miraculously versatile white wine, perfect to serve with white meats like veal (particularly Wiener schnitzel), pork, poultry, shellfish, and seafood.

Chenin Blanc (medium-body)
This grape is refreshing enough to enhance the flavor of anything that swims, especially more full-bodied fish such as salmon and sea bass. It also pairs beautifully with Asian dishes containing ginger, soy sauce, garlic, and honey, as well as American dishes with veal, pork, or any light meat poultry. Chenin Blanc is the grape in a wine called Vouvray, which is also available in a sparkling wine by the same name that does double duty with fried foods, egg dishes, and even salads.

Albariño (medium-body)
Spain's great white wine with refreshing acidity and lots of fruity aromas can marry with shellfish and seafood as easily as poultry, veal, and pork. I remember this wine by thinking, "Al Pacino," or "albino."

Viognier (full-body)
High alcohol, high acid white from France and California packed with flavors of apricots and peaches, pairs with medium-weight fish like salmon, halibut, sea bass, and lobster, as well as chicken, duck, pork, and veal.

Out of the Box Red Wines

Chinon and St. Nicholas de Bourgeuil (light-body)
Made from Cabernet Franc, one of the grapes that goes into the formidable Bordeaux blend, this refreshing, fruity wine goes with all delicate, as well as medium dishes like ham and chicken. My

memory trigger for Chinon is a woman's hairstyle pulled back in a bun at the nape of the neck, a chignon. For St. Nicholas de Bourgueil just think "St. Nicholas," or "boy, oh boy" for Bourgueil, which is the abbreviated name of the wine.

Chianti (light- to medium-body)

Made, as most Tuscan wines are, from the Sangiovese grape, Chianti is a low-tannin palate pleaser that you should dust off and bring back into the repertoire because it is versatile enough to be served with everything from pizza and pasta to calamari and sausage. Its refreshing acidity makes it the perfect partner for any high acid tomato or pesto-based sauce. If the wine label says simply "Chianti" it's light-bodied, but Chianti Riserva or Gran Riserva are medium-bodied. Keep in mind that California is now producing Sangiovese and Sangiovese blended with Cabernet, Merlot, or Syrah, and the results are delicious!

Rioja (light- to medium-body)

This Spanish wine is experiencing a renaissance due to modern wine-making techniques that are wowing consumers worldwide. So bring Rioja front and center as a delicious food-friendly wine with its good acidity, fruitiness, appealing oak flavors, and moderate tannin level. It tastes wonderful not only with traditional paella but with pork, veal, ham, and poultry. Rioja-Crianza is light-bodied, but Rioja Riserva and Gran Riserva are medium-bodied wines.

Beaujolais Cru (medium-body)

Emanating from ten specific villages (or "Crus"), these fruity reds are great bridge wines and can span the gap between fish, chicken, and veal dishes.

Malbec (full-body)

While this grape plays a cameo role in the red Bordeaux blend, it has a starring role as the sole performer in Argentina's fruity and tannic red. It's a wonderful stand-in for Cabernet because it is a tannic wine, especially good with fatty cuts of beef and all lamb dishes. To help remember Malbec, know that "mal" means bad in several languages . . . so think of "bad Becky."

Three Bridges to Bliss

I have three favorite bridge wines for a group of people who are eating wildly different kinds of foods and who only want to drink one bottle of wine. Pinot Noir is my all-time favorite bridge wine. It goes with every cuisine, every ingredient, so it gets along with everyone, and goes with everything. Next time you're in a food and wine pairing pinch, think Pinot. Shiraz has more spicy and peppery pizzazz, so substitute this wine when some of your friends are having dishes whose ingredients include spices or condiments that heat up the mouth. This juicy wine will offset the heat and cool down their palates with every sip.

Champagne and Beer

It's a searingly hot day, and the backyard picnic you've planned is underway. Your wife has just made her famous Southern Fried Chicken, your sister-in-law has shown up with her Creole Jambalaya, and your neighbor has made Texas Chili. The men are craving an icy beer, and all the ladies want a cool glass of white wine. What to serve? Champagne or sparkling wine.

Champagne, sparkling wine, and beer provide the same kind of "prickly" palate sensation that is refreshing and the perfect complement to fried food. I'm not suggesting opening a bottle of expensive vintage Champagne to enjoy with your corn dogs at the county fair, but, if the mood strikes and the wallet is able, the pairing would be ideal, flavor-wise. My personal credo: "When in doubt, drink Champagne."

I'm a big fan of the Italian reds, Barbera d'Alba and Barbera d'Asti, soft, easy drinking fruit bombs. Both are made from the same grape, Barbera, but grow in neighboring areas, Alba and Asti. But you can ditch the vino babble about long wine names and just ask for Barbera. I remember this wine by thinking of the woman's name, Barbara, and then go further with a whole sentence: Barbara is ready for her close-up. That's how I remember this wine doesn't need aging, aerating, or decanting, but is ready to drink tonight. It also has great acidity and low tannin, which makes it ideal to stand up to high acid tomato- and pesto-based sauces.

Barbera is a must when you eat Italian and need a bridge wine, because it's hard to find California Pinot Noir or Australian Shiraz in an Italian restaurant—that would be like trying to order a steak at a macrobiotic place. When in Rome, do as the Romans do.

Challenging Marriages

In the life of every couple there are problems and hurdles that crop up and must be addressed to avoid any unseemly outbursts. If you know, for example, that your great-aunt Mabel and your cousin Irving don't get along, you'd never seat them next to each other as dinner companions. The same thing is true with food and wine: There are certain components that make life difficult rather than delicious.

The Double "A" Dilemma

You ordered an artichoke salad, and your companion ordered asparagus. Do you recall the wine you ordered and the nightmarish result when you took a bite of your appetizer and a sip of your wine? Why did that happen?

Artichokes and asparagus by their very nature are extremely difficult to pair with wine. Eating artichokes is like adding a sweetener to your wine because part of its chemical content is cynarin, an acid that creates a sweet taste in the mouth. Similarly, asparagus, with its phosphorus and mercaptan, transforms a princely wine into a frog.

Some purists actually recommend not drinking any wine at all when eating these two foods in order to avoid taste destruction. Of course, the Wine Diva would never recommend not having wine in this or any scenario: Where there's a Wine Diva, there's a way. Just make sure that you select a light-bodied, unoaked, lightly flavored wine like Sauvignon Blanc or Pinot Grigio.

The Egg and I

Eggs may be a perfect food, but not when it comes to wine. The thick yellow yolk acts like a shield between your taste buds and the wine. The best way to cut through the creamy yolk that coats your palate is via unoaked white wines. Their high acidity scours and cleans the palate so you can taste the next bite of food. So with eggs reach for Champagne and sparkling wine, Sauvignon Blanc, Pinot Grigio, and Riesling, or a Pinot Noir if you prefer red.

Salad Daze

The Wine Diva will be blunt: It's not easy being green. Between the high chlorophyll content in lettuce and the vinegar in dressing, green salads are one of the trickiest dishes with which to share a bottle of wine. Chlorophyll clobbers the fine taste of wine, while vinegar robs wine of its fruitiness and flavor, making it astringent and completely unpleasant. (The exception is balsamic vinegar, which is sweet and nutty, and can actually contribute to the flavor of wine. Or substitute lemon or orange juice for vinegar in the dressing to be in balance with the lemony acidity of the refreshing white wine you will be enjoying.)

If you're faced with the challenge of selecting a wine to serve with a salad dressed in a vinaigrette, consider:

- **White wine or champagne vinaigrette:** Choose a light bodied, unoaked white wine, such as a Sauvignon Blanc, Muscadet, or Chablis.

- **Red wine or balsamic vinaigrette:** Choose a light- to medium-bodied red wine, such as a Pinot Noir or Chinon.

I recently came across two more radical and, I think, clever and creative solutions from a talented chef. First, you can vary the "greens" by using low-chlorophyll endive or radicchio or peppery arugula or watercress. The milder green lettuces, such as Boston or red oak, taste fine with a Sauvignon Blanc or Pinot Grigio. Second, instead of vinaigrette, try a wine reduction to dress your salads. Simply warm olive oil in a saucepan with whatever flavorings (garlic, onion, herbs) you choose and then slowly add wine. Let it cook for up to an hour until the wine is reduced to a thick syrup consistency. Cool before using on salad. Drink the same wine you used in the dressing and it will enhance your dining pleasure.

The Cheese Stands Alone

Surprisingly, certain cheeses are not always perfect foils for wine. How to order wine appropriately for the cheese course?

Goat Cheeses
(Chevre, Montrachet, Caprino)

Highly acidic goat cheese calls for higher-acid wine for balance, so look for Pinot Noir, Merlot, Barbera, or Chinon. If you prefer white wine, you can choose the traditional Sauvignon Blanc, Pinot Grigio, and Sancerre or the more "off-road" Riesling from Alsace, Germany, and Australia, Albariño from Spain, and Grüner Veltliner from Austria.

Mild, Soft Cheeses (Mozzarella)

This subtly flavored cheese needs a soft-spoken partner with no oaky flavors to overpower it. Reach for Italian wines like Pinot Grigio, Soave, Orvieto, Verdicchio, Arneis, Fiano, or Greco.

More Flavorful, Soft Cheeses (Brie, Camembert, Pont l'Eveque, Reblochon)

Tannic red wines destroy creamier cheeses, so enjoy these with medium-bodied, less tannic reds like Pinot Noir, Shiraz, Merlot, Côtes du Rhône, Rioja, Chianti, and Beaujolais Cru or older reds like a mature red Burgundy or a Chianti or Rioja Riserva that have had some bottle time to soften their tannins. If you prefer whites, try full-bodied California Chardonnay, white Burgundy, or white Bordeaux.

Blue Cheeses (Stilton, Maytag Blue, Bleu d'Auvergne)

These flavor-packed cheeses go exceptionally well with sweet white wines like Sauternes, Barsac,

Coteaux du Layon, sweet sherries from Spain, and late-harvest sweet Alsatian Pinot Gris, and especially well with Ruby Port, traditionally served with Stilton and pears all over England.

Smoked Cheeses
(Gouda, Cheddar, Mozzarella)

A definite challenge, owing to the smoky quality compounded by the flavor of the cheese, but not impossible. Good matches are spicy Alsatian Gewürztraminer for a white wine or spicy Australian Shiraz, Zinfandel, or Syrah if you prefer reds.

Hard Cheese (Pecorino di Pienza,
Parmigiano Reggiano, Pecorino di Tartufo)

Order or serve a fruity red with good acidity and moderate tannin, because a very tannic wine will clash with the pronounced saltiness in these cheeses and make the wine seem bitter, which is the old S Factor coming back to haunt you. Moreover, Parmesan is laden with umami, which also needs a less tannic wine partner. So consider Chianti and other Sangiovese-based reds, as well as Pinot Noir, red Burgundies, Shiraz, or Merlot.

Hard, Flavorful Cheese (Cheddar,
Aged Provolone, Aged Goat Cheese)

Fruity, medium-bodied reds kill flavorful cheeses, so this is when you bring out the big guns— full-bodied wines like Cabernet, red Bordeaux, Chateauneuf-du-Pape, Malbec, Zinfandel, Amarone, and Barolo.

The Icing on the Cake

You've made barbecue, or you've ordered a spicy Malaysian meal and ended it with a cheese plate. You've experimented and found the perfect wines to complement the meal so far. Now, perhaps, you're starting to think about dessert. As always, there are some guidelines to consider, but first and foremost is the fact that desserts—at least in the United States—are sweet, and sweets generally lose their appeal when paired with dry wines. But there are delicious dessert wines that complement sweets beautifully, and are well worth investigating. Permit the Wine Diva to introduce:

- **Port:** There is an old Portuguese saying: "All wine would be port, if it could." Alas, it cannot—only certain grapes grown in the Duoro Valley in Portugal can be called port. This velvety, lush wine is produced in two broad categories: vintage (1 percent of the entire production) and non-vintage. Vintage port is made only in exceptional years and is the "reserve" wine of the dessert world. Non-vintage ports, like non-vintage Champagnes, are a blend of several vintages, and come in a myriad of styles and price points from simple Ruby Ports to the more complex Tawny Ports that have been aging for ten, twenty, or thirty years. Port is a delicious way to cap off a meal, especially when served with rich chocolate and coffee desserts, and with nuts.

- **Sauternes:** Nectar of the Gods, if it ever existed, this magnificent blend of Sauvignon Blanc and Semillon is the result of a bad thing—Botrytis—gone good. Also called Noble Rot, Botrytis is a fungus that infects the grapes and produces a higher sugar and acid content, as well as the lush flavors of this staggeringly delicious (and often staggeringly expensive) wine. Enjoy French Sauternes (or their less-expensive next-door neighbors Barsac, Cadillac, Loupiac, and St. Croix du Mont) with apple, pear, peach, and apricot-based desserts, as well as pound cake. This style of lush, sweet wine is also being made in California and Australia.

- **Late Harvest Riesling from Alsace and California:** Sweet, supple, and lower in alcohol than Port, this lovely dessert wine matches well with crème brûleé, custard, and flan, and apricot or peach, as well as citrus-based pies and tarts.

- **Champagne** goes best with fruit-based desserts or sweets with nutty ingredients. The pleasant, refreshing acidity in the fruit is echoed by the brisk acidity in the Champagne; and nutty ingredients in a dessert echo the biscuity, breadbox flavors that can develop as Champagnes spend many years lying on their sides with the wine in contact with the sediment.

There are many other wonderful dessert wines to satisfy a sweet tooth, including Coteaux de Layon, Bonnezeaux, and Quarts de Chaume from France, Tokay Aszu from Hungary, Madeira from Portugal, Marsala from Italy,

Breakneck Bottles

 The stylish way to open a bottle of Champagne is by *sabrage* or sabering. You literally decapitate the bottle with a saber. But with port a rather less swashbuckling approach is adopted. Port, if it has been in the bottle for many years, forms a tremendous amount of crust. If the cork is too old and crumbly to be drawn out in the usual way, the neck of the bottle may be gripped with red hot tongs, then immediately wrapped in a cold damp cloth. The sudden change in temperature causes the neck to break clean off.

sweet sherries from Spain, and late harvest Pinot Gris from Alsace—experiment to discover matches made in Wine Diva heaven.

The Joy of Ex . . . perimenting: It's All in Good Taste

There is never any substitute for firsthand experience, which is why I heartily urge you to experiment in the pairing of food and wine, using my guidelines. Taste never lies, so to see what happens when you serve a big California or Australian Chardonnay with a spicy, umamiful light meal—do a taste test and decide how *you* like the combination.

Whether you're faced with the simplest or most challenging of food and wine pairings, just remember to wear those white cuffs, smile, and enjoy. The way you look and the way you feel will be perfectly paired, and wonderful.

The Wine Diva promises.

Wine in *Restaurants*

H ere it is—Saturday night and you and your spouse are going out to dinner with friends. The restaurant could be your favorite Chinese, a moderate neighborhood haunt, or a gastronomic Mecca. When it's time to order wine, do you, like a school child who has not done the homework, pray you're not called on? Or do you confidently say, "Yes, I'd like to see the list."

No situation involving wine provokes more angst than selecting a wine in a restaurant. Here in the pleasant atmosphere of a fine dining establishment, with an audience of family, friends, or business associates, your wine savvy is on the line. Are you up to the challenge of choosing a wine with confidence and panache? Read the following chapter, swirl it around in your mind, and never suffer ordering anxiety again!

In the Beginning

Deciphering the List

While there is no foolproof way to help you decode the list and give you clues to choosing from perhaps hundreds of listed wines, I can give you some helpful hints.

A wine list is usually organized in one of three ways:

1. **By country.** This approach is common and yet to many Americans not very helpful, since 75 percent of us drink California and order by grape variety. It also discourages trying wines from less well-known countries such as South Africa or Argentina. If these sleeper wines were intermixed by type with their American counterparts, you'd probably be more encouraged to try them.

2. **By grape variety.** This is a user-friendly method since the vast majority of Americans order wine by grape variety—Cabernet Sauvignon, Chardonnay, etc. Ideally these varieties are listed within general categories of white or red in order from light-bodied at the top to full-bodied at the bottom. For example:

WHITE WINES:	RED WINES:
Pinot Grigio	Pinot Noir
Riesling	Merlot
Sauvignon Blanc	Shiraz/Syrah
Pinot Gris	Zinfandel
Chardonnay	Cabernet Sauvignon

3. **By flavor profile.** This is the most helpful organization of all. It is a good first step in helping people pair wines with food by putting together all the wines on the list— regardless of country of origin or grape variety—according to their flavor profiles and weight. Headings such as "light and zesty," "medium, round, and fruity," or "big and bold" point diners in the right direction when they are trying to figure out what wines go best with what dishes.

The Sommelier

If you are seated at a table and someone other than your waiter asks if you'd like to see the wine list, that means a special person is dedicated to such service: the sommelier (So-mahl-YEAH). The name comes from the French word *somme*, which can mean "burden." The sommelier has the "burden" of purchasing the restaurant's wines, advising on food and wine pairings, and serving wines to patrons on a full-time basis. Some sommeliers wear a pretentious uniform, sometimes with an odd-looking apron and a shallow silver cup called a *tastevin* (wine taster) hanging on a chain. You may also notice a pin on a label signifying a wine degree. Others wear business clothes so they stand apart from the wait staff. Whatever the attire, the sommelier is your wine list navigator.

Note: Although I hear the expression far too often, it's not hip to refer to the sommelier as the wine steward. Back in the days when women traveled to Europe with their wardrobes in steamer trunks, people were attended by a wine steward. In the same way, decades ago people were served on airplanes by air hostesses, then stewardesses— today most people call them flight attendants.

The sommelier is there to help you, so take advantage of the help. The best approach is to give the sommelier a hint as to your preferences by saying, "I like California Cabernets, so which of these Italian wines would likely suit my taste?" Or consider asking the sommelier, "Which are your favorites?" or "Which of these wines are ready to drink now?" Ask about wines or wine terms you don't recognize. "What can you tell me about this wine?" is a great line to use to flatter the sommelier (or savvy waiter) into sharing some

inside information about a
wine. No matter how the
conversation goes, engaging
the sommelier in your
selection gives you a better

Under duress to find a bargain? Not when you can order Auxey-Duresses (ox-ay dure-ESS), a white Burgundy.

outcome than the alternative of closing your eyes
and pointing randomly at the list.

What if you don't know French or Italian at
all, your Spanish is pretty rusty, and your German
comes from old war movies? You might naturally
try to avoid speaking to the sommelier for fear of
stumbling over the pronunciation of foreign wine
names. There is a foolproof way to get around
this. Say you are looking over the wine list and
would like to try an Alsatian Riesling but the
name is something like Grand Cru Zinnkoepflé.
Just point to this wine on the list and let the
waiter or sommelier pronounce it for you. Don't
be surprised if he also mangles the name. That
doesn't reflect on his wine knowledge, only that
he bungled his way through the same language
classes that you did.

Whether you are dealing with a sommelier or
a waiter, three bits of information help the staff
find the right wine for you and your companions:

- *The food you have ordered.* Guide the
  sommelier or waiter by offering some food
  pairing cues such as, "We are all having the
  lamb tonight," or "We have ordered a range of
  dishes from the chicken special to roast lamb,
  and wonder what would be delicious with
  everything."

- *The price you would like to pay.* Don't be
  embarrassed to indicate what you would like
  to spend. If you have $25 in mind, there is no
  sense in getting a recommendation for a '94

Meritage at $100 and up. "What would you recommend at about $40?" is okay to say. If you are shy about mentioning price aloud or in front of guests or colleagues, point to a $40 bottle on the list and say "What would you suggest at this level?" This should clue the waiter as to the price range you're in.

- *Your degree of wine knowledge.* If you know virtually nothing, say so. If you are in the advanced beginners class you might say something like, "I love Italian wines but last week my friend ordered a Bardolino, and it was too light for my taste. What do you think I'd enjoy more?" If you are feeling experimental, you might say "What wines do you think are terrific—other than Cabernet or Chardonnay?" Then you are not only flattering your advisor, but possibly discovering a great bargain.

In the end it is you, not the sommelier or waiter, who has to be satisfied. Show a collaborative spirit and you'll get great results.

A note on tipping the sommelier: The tip you leave for your meal includes a portion for the sommelier, but if he or she has rendered service "above and beyond" you may want to consider an extra monetary thank-you. Offering you an old wine from the cellar that is not on the list would qualify. Such extra service would especially apply if you have brought your own wine and the corkage charge has been modest or nonexistent. (Five or ten dollars should be sufficient.)

Pace Yourself

If you plan to have wine served while you are waiting for your food, don't order a glass of

Chardonnay or Cabernet on autopilot. These are not the best wines to have on an empty stomach. You should be in first gear with a wine that has *modest alcohol* containing 10 to 12 percent compared to California Chardonnay and Cabernet with a whopping 13 to 15 percent alcohol. The difference between 10 percent and 15 percent is 50 percent more alcohol! Two glasses of the latter could mean a hangover instead of a happy buzz. So move out slowly.

Another hallmark of a good wine to drink on its own is that it should have relatively high lemony/juicy acidity for a refreshing, pleasant, lively taste in your mouth. Such wines are also wonderful with first course appetizers because they help you pace yourself for the big reds to come.

Now for the Specifics

American white wines that are good for starters include Riesling, Sauvignon Blanc, and Fumé Blanc (the latter is also made from the Sauvignon Blanc grape but the wine has a kiss of oak flavor). The best reds would be Pinot Noir and Sangiovese.

French entries for aperitif white wines are Riesling and Pinot Blanc from Alsace, Chablis from Burgundy, Muscadet and Sancerre from the Loire Valley. Red wines would include Chinon, St Nicholas de Bourgeuil, Côtes du Rhône, and Beaujolais-Villages—a big step up in quality from Beaujolais Nouveau.

In casual Italian restaurants, there will always be the ubiquitous Pinot Grigio, Soave, Verdicchio, or Frascati by

Corny St. Joseph lives with crowds in a hermitage helps you remember three good value Rhône reds: Cornes, St. Joseph, and Crozes-Hermitage.

the glass. More upscale venues will usually offer by the glass Italian Sauvignon Blanc, which has much more flavor than its mild-mannered cousins. Lighter reds include Dolcetto, Bardolino, and Valpolicella.

Australia weighs in with its juicy white Riesling and young Semillon from the Hunter Valley. If you prefer red, opt for a Pinot Noir or the country's flagship red, Shiraz.

Don't overlook the vast selection of sparkling wines produced in virtually every wine producing region in the world, including Champagne and Cremant de Loire from France; Cava from Spain, Sekt from Germany, and Prosecco from Italy. Most sparkling wines are relatively low in alcohol and a refreshing—not to mention elegant and festive—start to any meal.

Riesling: Misunderstood but Magical

To me, Riesling is the greatest white wine, both as an aperitif and as a food partner. But it's a wine that is completely misunderstood. I get so frustrated when someone rejects even trying it because they are convinced "it's too sweet." Riesling comes in such a wide range of styles, from very dry to opulently sweet that there is a taste for everyone and every food. No wine is more refreshing and boasts lower alcohol levels. All Rieslings from Alsace are dry (except the small percentage that say "Late Harvest" and "SGN," which signify wines that are sweet). Also, Rieslings from California, Australia, Austria, and South Africa are dryer than their German counterparts.

But it's well worth looking for a dry German Riesling on the menu. They still haven't dispelled their "sweetish" image, so the dry versions can be a bargain on the wine list compared to their counterparts from other regions.

Besides asking the sommelier, here are two ways to ferret out delicious, food-friendly dry Rieslings.

- Look for the term Riesling "Kabinett" on the wine list. (Kabinett connotes a level of quality in the German wine hierarchy.) I remember this by thinking Riesling sounds a little like "wrestling." Kabinett sounds like the word "cabinet." And sometimes I have to "wrestle open a cabinet door" in the kitchen.

- Look for Riesling "trocken." Trocken means dry.

The First Food Court

For centuries it was customary for the French nobility to dine in private at one another's palaces and chateaux in the countryside and at their *hotels particulaires* (townhouse mansions) in Paris. The aristocracy didn't mingle with the bourgeoisie in inns, taverns, or cafés. In 1780, the enterprising young Duke de Chartres decided to prop up his dwindling fortune by launching a novel real estate scheme. His Palais Royale was remodeled into an unprecedented commercial extravaganza. The garden was excavated to create a subterranean cavern where the duke rented out space for entertainment such as chess clubs, billiard halls, gambling dens, private clubs, music halls, and brothels. The arcades and colonnades at ground level he rented out to retail shops, cafés, art galleries, bookstalls, and that newest of inventions, restaurants. The upper floors included private apartments rented to impoverished aristocrats. Thus below ground the first "multiplex" entertainment center was created and above ground the first shopping mall and food court! It was in this exhilarating environment that the classes mixed.

One of the restaurants established before the French Revolution in the Palais Royal is still going strong today in its original location. It is called Le Grand Vefour and is an elegant restaurant, rating three prized stars in the Michelin guide, the Bible of restaurant ratings.

Money Matters

Here are ways to find good values on a wine list whether you drink a little or a lot or whether you drink the "usual suspects" like Cabernet and Chardonnay or are more adventurous.

How Many Bottles Do I Need to Order?

Assuming you are going to have an appetizer and an entrée, figure on a half bottle of wine per guest. That may sound like a lot, but it amounts to about two and a half glasses of wine per person for the entire evening. Even if some guests start with a cocktail, most switch to wine with their food. So with four people you still need to order two bottles, usually one white and one red. Which wine to have first? Remember, white before red, and young before old. White wine is usually a good bet to start with because most people begin a meal with a light appetizer. When you are a group of six people, order a mix of three bottles of wine. This may be an opportunity to try several different wines much as you might try something different on someone else's plate. Obviously, if you know your guests prefer to have only one glass of wine throughout their meal, ordering by the glass or half-bottle is smart. But if you underestimate your consumption, you'll end up paying more.

How Much to Spend

You want to pick a fairly priced bottle of wine from the menu at a nice restaurant, but you are not sure how to do this. What you should spend is entirely personal, but a good rule of thumb is "the extra person at the table." If in this restaurant an average appetizer and entrée add up to $40, it's about what a nice bottle should cost. Some restaurants wildly overcharge for their wines and others offer real bargains. If you know what a wine sells for in the store, a fair wine list price is about two and a half times that. Therefore $20 at the store becomes $50 at the restaurant. On the other hand some restaurants want to sell a lot of wine and price them well—less than two times retail. Reward these restaurants (and yourself) with your patronage.

One easy way to gauge whether you're being gouged is to memorize the store price of a common wine or two. Then, when you see it on the wine list, you can check out the markup. It should not be any more than two and a half to three times the retail price.

There is an exception to this guideline: If a wine is scarce—from a prized vintage, perhaps, or a cult wine—the restaurant may charge much more. Expect anything up to 600 percent! Remember, these are the kinds of wines that rarely, if ever, reach a retail shelf. You can only get them at restaurants, so expect to pay for the privilege of enjoying these rare jewels.

When Price Is an Issue

Whether your company is picking up the tab or not, you have a budget in mind but don't want to mention it in front of your guests. How do you ask for help when money is a factor? The question of price can be sticky, but here's how to get around it. Since you generally start out with lighter fare for the first course, open the wine list and look for a light bodied white wine like Sauvignon Blanc in a price range you are comfortable with. Point to the price of this wine, not the wine name, and say to the sommelier, "I was wondering about this wine for our first course." The sensitive sommelier will either compliment you on your choice or suggest something else in approximately the same range, with your guests none the wiser. The sommelier will also have a price clue as you consider reds and, unless he/she has a tin ear, will suggest additional wines in the same price and quality range. It's the sommelier's job to listen carefully.

What if you are especially fond of a certain grape—say Chardonnay—but all the California Chardonnays on the wine list are beyond your budget? Simply look for the same grape from a lower profile geographic area—perhaps Australia, Chile, or South Africa. It's akin to clothes

Musical Chairs and Eating Family Style

In the 1700s the nobility of pre-Revolutionary France ate heavy dinners with everything served at once: four soups, four fish dishes, four *pièce de résistance* roasts, thirty-six side dishes, and a dozen desserts. Serving all the food at once was called service *"à la Francaise."* Dinners were lengthy affairs and guests seated themselves as they pleased. Since the tables were so laden with food, the guests could not talk across the table but only to the person to their left and right, thus talking *"tête-à-tête,"* head to head. When finished conversing, guests rose, strolled around the room, and sat down wherever they pleased.

With the nobility virtually wiped out during the French Revolution, many of the great French chefs fled to England and became chefs to the English aristocracy. Thus throughout the 1800s fine dining in England reflected the same heavy French-inspired menus accompanied by the same celebrated wines from Bordeaux, Burgundy, the Rhône, and Champagne. Dinners lasted five hours, only now served *"à la Russe"*—that is, in an organized fashion, appetizer through dessert, after the fashion of the Russian court started by Catherine the Great. Everyone was seated according to strict protocol and did not change places.

Today, we eat *"à la Russe"* and sit at the table *"à la Francaise."*

shopping: There is the Donna Karan designer line, but get out of the high rent boutique district and you can find the lower priced DKNY. You get a similar style at a fraction of the price.

You can often find a good deal in varietals that not as many people are familiar with—for example, Pinot Gris and Shiraz. If you order them instead of their higher priced counterparts (Chardonnay and Cabernet), you won't be disappointed and you'll leave the restaurant with more money in your wallet.

Is it a good strategy for picking a wine to order one of the least expensive wines at a great restaurant because you know the food will be fantastic and will make the wine seem better? Not at all. If budget is the problem, pick a less expensive restaurant! You probably wouldn't wear dime store jewelry with your best dress. After all, sips taken before or after the dish is served, and extra sips in between bites, easily outnumber those sips taken with food. For that reason, never choose a wine hoping the food will make it taste better. Pick a wine you know you will like, so you are sure to enjoy it.

The Smart Splurge

Let's say you are entertaining clients you'd like to impress and you can afford an expensive bottle. What should you do? Call the restaurant ahead of time to tell the sommelier you need a wine that will wow your guests. Do not, however, say, "Money is no object." Doing so signals that you have no knowledge of wine. The sommelier may be tempted to recommend an expensive, five year-old cult wine from Bordeaux for the sake of unadulterated "label worship" or a great wine (at a great price) that is far too young to drink. If your client knows a bit about wine and the sommelier takes this direction, they both might think you have more money than sense.

Instead, tell the sommelier that the evening is a special occasion and you would like his recommendation for a wine "ready to drink now." This approach has a number of benefits. First, you may save some money. Second, you will drink better. Third, your client will be wowed, just as you hope, because using the key words "ready to drink now" shows a lot of wine savvy. For the inside scoop on when wines are ready to drink, fast-forward to the 10 Percent Rule on pages 108–109.

Do Your Homework

A final thought about choosing a wine. If the dinner you are about to have in a restaurant is a big deal and you want to have more time to make your choices, call ahead and discuss the issue with the sommelier in the late morning or in the midafternoon when they have some free time. Also, the list is sometimes on the restaurant's Web site or else could be faxed. Ordinarily this is more effort than it's worth, but if you are about to spend several hundred dollars on wine, it could be time well spent.

Good Values for the Adventurous

There are great rewards if you are ready to be a little more experimental in your wine selection. The basic rule is that the less familiar the wine, the more likely it will be more fairly priced. Wines are brands just as fashion items are, and the famous ones carry a premium price. Our next challenge is to learn how to find the values when the wines are not household names.

Bargain Hunting in Burgundy

You'd like to find an affordable white Burgundy. On a casual wine list, if you want to pick a white Burgundy (made from Chardonnay), look for the recognizable standby Pouilly-Fuissé. At a more upscale restaurant, the number of white Burgundies is staggering, and sometimes the prices will have you reeling, so here is some help for your pocketbook.

- *The saints come marching in.* Several affordable white Burgundies start with Saint: St-Aubin, St-Veran, and St-Romain. You will generally find one of these "Saints" on the menu of a high-end restaurant.

- *It takes a village.* Remember that Burgundy is a veritable mosaic of tiny villages. The white wines from a group of villages called Macon-Villages generally cost less than the "Saints" mentioned above and are usually attractively priced on a wine list. You'll recognize these wines on a list because "Macon" always precedes the name of the tiny village. For example, Macon-Lugny, Macon-Vire. While they do not have the high profile of a Pouilly-Fuissé, they sometimes come close.

- *A generic prescription.* When the wine does not come from a specific village in Burgundy, it is simply called *Bourgogne Blanc* on the wine list, meaning generic white Burgundy. The sommelier usually cherry picks in order to find a good producer at a reasonable price in order to offer customers at least one white Burgundy under $30 a bottle.

Bargain Hunting in Bordeaux

You would like to order those wonderful Bordeaux reds with your meal, but they are so expensive. How can you choose wisely when the region is a patchwork quilt of areas and producers? Even though your dot-com ship didn't come in, it's often possible to find delicious Bordeaux on a menu for $35 to $45 a bottle—good value, high quality alternatives to the pricey classified growths. Ask the waiter or sommelier for wine recommendations using these ideas as guides:

- Choose wines from areas near or next to the famous areas. Examples for Merlot-based reds are (1) LaLande de Pomerol, which is next door to pricey Pomerol and (2) St-Emilion satellites that are vineyards surrounding high status St-Emilion. Conveniently, these include the suffix St-Emilion on their wine labels. For example, St-Georges-St-Emilion, Lussac-St-Emilion, and Montagne-St-Emilion. However, if you can't remember Pomerol and St-Emilion, don't worry. Just ask your server or sommelier to ferret out these bargains for you by letting them know you'd like a bottle of Bordeaux "from the next-door neighbors to the famous châteaux."

- Turn to substitute wines that can often pass for the more renowned and expensive growths. Choose second labels from great producers. Examples of Cabernet-based reds are: Carruades de Lafite from Lafite-Rothschild, and Bahans de Haut Brion from Haut Brion. A "second wine" almost always includes part of the name of the primary label. While these second wines were judged not good enough to be allowed into the *grand vins*, they give you a reasonably priced way to taste Bordeaux's expensive top wines and can be almost as good as the real deal. Don't worry if you don't know the names of the top wines. Simply ask the sommelier or waiter to recommend a Bordeaux "second label" to you.

- "Cru Bourgeois" and "petites châteaux" wines are amazing values. The former is an official category referring to almost 250 affordable wines one rung below the 61 top wines classified back in 1855. Some of my favorites in this group are Château d'Angludet, Phelan-Segur, and Château Potensac. The latter is the unofficial name covering thousands of wines that are reliable values.

- Choose a great wine in a so-so vintage (the year the grapes are harvested is the vintage of the wine).

- Ask for a lesser wine in a great vintage.

Rhône Wines

There are some really good values from this region in southern France, which produces super-expensive Syrah called Hermitage and Côte Rotie and blends called Châteauneuf-du-Pape.

Surrounding Hermitage and just across the river are three wines made from the same Syrah grape that goes into Hermitage, which are very good value for money: Crozes-Hermitage, Cornas, and Saint-Joseph.

Châteauneuf-du-Pape (a blend) is one of the best known wines of the Rhône Valley—but just across the river lies an area called Lirac, similar in character at half the price. Nearby Gigondas and many a well-made Côtes du Rhônes-Villages could also stand in for Châteauneuf-du-Pape at similar savings.

A Wine by Any Other Name

If you want a good value in California Cabernet and Cabernet-based Bordeaux style blends, also called Meritage (see page 40–42), certain top producers also make a second label. These wines are not "seconds" in the sense of damaged or unacceptable clothing. Instead, they're closer to a designer that has two separate lines, one high end, and one priced more affordably. So second label wines are quite good, a great value, and a secret to be shared.

Some you can easily remember because of the obvious connection between the names:

Top Wine	Second Label	Wine Type
Pride Mountain Napa Valley Reserve	Pride Mountain Napa Valley	Cabernet
Cain Five	Cain Cuvée	Meritage
Dalle Valle	Casa Dalle Valle	Cabernet
Others have a more subtle connection:		
Opus One	Overture (both musical terms)	Meritage
Arrowwood Reserve Speciale	Grand Archer (arrow and archer)	Cabernet
Some have a completely different name from the premium wine:		
Pahlmeyer	Jayson	Meritage
Joseph Phelps Napa Valley	Innasfree Napa Valley	Cabernet

Unfortunately, there is no rule to identify these second labels. The simplest way to find out is just ask if any of the wines on the list are "second labels" from top wineries.

What Wine to Order

Once you know what the table is ordering, pick a wine that "weighs in" with the food. (See Food and Wine, page 44.) In the white category, a light-bodied wine like Sauvignon Blanc pairs with light fare. An easy way to remember the type of light dishes this wine goes with is to think of the "Seven S's": salads, soups (without cream), seafood, shellfish, spicy, salty and smoky flavored foods. Other light, refreshing whites are:

- Muscadet, Pinot Blanc, and Chablis (France)

- Pinot Grigio, Vermentino, Verdicchio, Frascati, and Soave (Italy)

- Fumé Blanc (California)

Chardonnay is a medium- to full-bodied wine and works well with mediumweight foods like chicken, fish, and white meats like pork and veal. Remember, when these foods are cooked they are usually grilled, roasted, or broiled. All these cooking methods brown the outside, which caramelizes the juices inside. These caramel flavors in the food connect deliciously with the caramel, toasty flavors in oaked Chardonnay.

Other medium- to full-bodied whites that have some oaky flavors are: white Bordeaux (a Sauvignon Blanc/Semillon blend from France) and white Burgundy (made from the Chardonnay grape in France).

If you prefer, fresh, crisp, medium-bodied whites with no vanilla, butterscotch, or smoky flavors, choose from:

- Pinot Gris (Oregon and France)

- Sancerre and Pouilly Fumé (made from the Sauvignon Blanc grape, France)

- Arneis, Fiano, and Greco (Italy)

- Albariño and Rueda (Spain)

- Grüner Veltliner (Austria)

In the red category, for mediumweight foods like salmon, tuna, and pork, pick Pinot Noir, the best all-rounder. Delicious alternatives are Australian Shiraz, French red Burgundies made from Pinot Noir, as well as Syrah from France.

Ask for Cabernet and red Bordeaux for heavyweights like burgers, steaks, chops, lamb, and game. Or be color-blind if you'd really prefer a white, and order a full-bodied Chardonnay or white Burgundy, Chardonnay-Semillon blend, or a white Bordeaux.

Barbecued food and highly spiced dishes whether light-, medium-, or heavyweight need red wines that have refreshing acidity and gobs of fruit. Juicy acidity in a wine dampens the heat of the dish, and sweet fruit flavors offset the fire of BBQ sauce, dynamic spices, and seasonings. Look on the wine list for the following refreshing reds:

Try It, You'll Like It

You are in a casual restaurant with a two- to three-page wine list that is overly blessed with California Chardonnays and Cabernets. You know them, you like them. Why should you try something new if you're not sure you are going to like it?

If you never order anything but chicken and steak then perhaps you'll never be convinced to experiment. But if you are open to trying the food specials of the day, why not different wines? It's time to get off the comfort of the Cabernet and Chardonnay Highway (and the Pinot Grigio *autostrada*), head off onto the backroads, and explore! You can try so many interesting new wines on a wine list for $20 to $40. So, no more excuses—get off the beaten path, and you'll enjoy the scenery.

Zinfandel, Shiraz, Pinot Noir, and its French cousin red Burgundy and Syrah-based wines from California and the Rhône Valley in France.

In food and wine pairing, there are no rules, only preferences. But there's one maxim most wine educators seem to agree on: When in doubt, drink Champagne!

Champagne and sparkling wines have thirst-quenching effervescence that acts like a fire hose, cooling the flavors of spicy, salty, and smoky foods. Champagne's brisk, refreshing acidity also cuts through fried foods, egg dishes, and creamy ingredients. Finally, Champagne comes in light-, medium , and full-bodied styles to match the weight of the food. Just ask your waiter for the best meal partner.

Vintage Significance

You have enough trouble remembering PINs, passwords, phone numbers of friends, family, and clients, let alone birthdays of your nieces and nephews. Who can be expected to memorize good vintage years in order to get the best possible bottle of wine?

First, the good news: You really don't have to know about good versus bad vintage years to buy red wines from wine-producing regions like California, Australia, Chile, Argentina, and South Africa. These New World regions are generally warmer than Old World areas such as France and Germany, so year-to-year weather variation is much less significant—and so the quality of a particular vintage year is less important. California, for example, had a number of fine vintages throughout the 1990s.

European Old World wine growing regions, on the other hand, are cooler and sometimes grapes have to struggle to ripen. These unpredictable weather conditions result in tremendous vintage variation and therefore in wine quality from one year to the next. To underscore this point: France and Italy have had only six great red wine vintage years in the past twenty years: 1982, 1985, 1988, 1990, 1997, and 2000. Consider them carefully whenever they appear on lists. Here are two ways to help remember the really good years in the Old World:

- Make a cheat sheet with numbers 82, 85, 88, 90, 97, 00 using a stick-on label attached to your most used credit card. (Make sure you don't cover the magnetic strip!)

- Create your own mnemonic device using birth years of your children or spouse, such as Megan (born in 1982), Charlie (1988), or Kate (1990), as reminders of the good years in more ways than one.

Time in the Bottle—The 10 Percent Rule

You don't want to order a wine that's either past its peak or be tempted to pay for a big bottle before it's ready to drink. What you need is a simple way to assess the drinkability or age worthiness of the most popular red and white wines. In general, the costlier the wine, the longer its life span and the more age it needs to reach its prime. Knowing that, I came up with the 10 percent rule. If a wine on the restaurant's wine list is $30, order it if it's three years or less from the vintage. (The vintage is simply the year the grapes were harvested.) For example, a $30 bottle of Sauvignon Blanc, Pinot Grigio, Pinot Blanc, or Beaujolais-Villages on a list in 2006 should be from the 2003 vintage or later. Bottles older than

2003 will be past their peak of freshness and will taste pretty dull and lifeless.

At around $50 a bottle, your favorites—Chardonnay, Pinot Noir, Merlot, Syrah, Zinfandel, and Cabernet Sauvignon—are ready for their close-up and can be enjoyed immediately. These are "drink me now" wines that can be enjoyed young but have a life span of about five years during which time they don't change and get more complex. Apply the 10 percent rule. The $50 bottle on the wine list in 2006 should be from the 2001 vintage or later. See how easy it is.

Only a fraction of the wines in the world are age worthy for a decade or more. Cabernet is in this league. (Turn to Storing Your Wine on page 166 for a broader list.)

- Pass up premium Cabernets (and Cabernet-based blends from France called red Bordeaux) at $80 to $120 unless they are at least three to five years old. Any younger, and the wines offer little complexity and will leave your mouth feeling "dried out" from astringent tannins. So if the list has only current vintages in this price range, save your money and order a less expensive wine that's ready to drink now.

- Close your eyes to Cabernets or red Bordeaux in the super-premium category at $125 and up unless they are six to eight years old. You won't impress wine savvy clients, friends, or family if you order these wines from a recent vintage. Quite the contrary, you'll actually be showing them you don't know much about wine and are just forking over the big bucks because of what is called "label worship." It takes six to eight years to reach a point at which these wines start showing off their complex aromas and flavors, and have softer tannin. So don't waste money on an expensive bottle before it's ready for prime time.

Beyond the Wine List

Wine lists are living, evolving creations. Sometimes, after carefully considering our choices and selecting the perfect wine, you'll be told, "We are out of that." Try not to be annoyed. Instead, use this as an opportunity to ask, "Are there wines in stock not on the list?" This may occur if at the time of printing the new list a handful of older wines, soon to be out of stock, were not included in the new printing. These may be treasures that only the sommelier knows about.

Remembering the Wine

You may have gotten some wonderful recommendations from sommeliers—but often the problem is that you can't remember the wines after that magic dinner is over. Here's a suggestion: Ask for the sommelier's business card, and that he or she make a note of the wine you ordered. If no business card is available, offer the back of your own. You'll be able to make a record of the wine so you won't have to rely on memory alone. For such good service, you'll want to show your gratitude. Instead of adding the sommelier's gratuity to your credit card charge, offer cash to express your very personal thanks for picking such a perfect wine for your dinner. This is sure to impress the sommelier, and you can be assured the next time you're back, you'll be remembered. And while it's a nice feeling to be recognized when you return to a restaurant, what may also ensue is the sommelier mentioning a handful of his or her personal favorite wines available in such limited quantity that they are not on the wine list.

Bringing Your Own Bottle

You have a wonderful bottle of fine wine reserved for a special occasion. Instead of cooking at home, you decide to go to a restaurant for the celebration, and you'd love to enjoy that bottle of wine. Some restaurants welcome guests with their own wine, some do it if asked, and some absolutely forbid it. Be sure to call ahead to save any awkward moments. Ask to speak to the manager or the owner and say, "I'd very much appreciate it if I could bring a bottle that is special to me—a '94 Mondavi that we bought on a trip to Napa. Of course, I am happy to pay the corkage fee." Don't be afraid to ask what the corkage will be. The fee can range from $10 to $25 a bottle, depending whether you are at a casual, fine, or top restaurant. If you arrive with your bottle unannounced, you may wind up paying a corkage that is a corker!

A couple of things to avoid:

- Don't bring a commonly available wine. It signals that you are just trying to save a buck.

- Never, ever bring a wine already on their wine list.

Remember that you saved a lot of money by bringing your own wine but the waiter should not be penalized for your astuteness. Figure a fair price for your wine and adjust the gratuity

Amorous Julie sat on a chair and passed wind. A flurry of cherubs helped Morgan reign as king in Brouilly and Cote de Brouilly.

The ten villages that produce a red wine called Beaujolais cru are: Saint-Amour, Julienas, Chenas, Moulin-a-Vent, Fleurie, Chiroubles, Morgon, Regnie, Brouilly, Cote de Brouilly.

appropriately to include 15 to 20 percent for your server. And since a restaurant relies heavily on the profit from its wine list, you shouldn't make a habit of abusing the privilege.

Class Wine by the Glass

Wine by the glass has changed in recent years from "house red and house white" to a much more robust selection of good to great wines. Ordering wine by the glass is no longer a way to have a cheap wine, but now an opportunity to taste unfamiliar wines without having to buy a whole bottle. Here are a few suggestions:

- Treat the wines-by-the-glass list as a tasting menu. If you and your dining companions can agree, order a variety of wines by the glass and taste all around.

- Ask for an extra empty glass. You will be able to share and as a side benefit you will be able to allow the wine fill to be at the proper level in order to swirl the contents (about a third full) while still getting the value of the full glass sold.

- If you are with a group of six or more, ask for a tasting pour (generally an ounce to an ounce and a half) of two or three wines by the glass. If the restaurant sees that you are about to order a significant amount of wine, they likely will accommodate your request. This will also help you decide which wine the group might like by the bottle.

- If there are wines by the glass that are also sold by the bottle, compare prices. Wines by the glass should be one quarter of the price of a full bottle. If they are significantly above this amount, wines by the glass are overpriced.

- Ask when the bottle used for the wine by the glass you are considering was opened. Be especially wary on a Monday if you are at a casual restaurant. Wines that were corked on Saturday night will have lost much of their aroma and freshness by Monday night. This shouldn't be an issue at fine restaurants where the staff is taught to retaste all the open bottles before every service period to ensure they are fresh.

- Try to avoid the extremes of the price range. The cheap stuff may be truly awful and the top of the line may be ordered so infrequently that the bottle from which it is poured may have been opened four to five days ago and will taste lifeless.

The Last Word

Let's say you are enjoying the wine that you selected. You're in a group with some knowledgeable wine enthusiasts who talk in "vino babble" about the wine's "good vein of acidity," or the "ripe, polished tannins," and "brambly fruit with a hint of lead pencil and *pain grillé*." They are talking about *your* wine and you feel a degree of parental pride. You want to make one intelligent remark about the wine without getting in over your head.

"Don't play that game" may be the first thought that comes to your mind, and it's a perfect acceptable stance. But if you feel you must comment, here is one sentence that will have them nodding their heads in recognition of your discerning palate. Simply say, "This wine seems *well balanced* and has a *great finish*." What did you just say?

You liked the wine and couldn't find anything to complain about. If it was a white wine, you didn't experience nostril-enlarging acidity that would mean it was too tart. There was no searing heat in the back of your throat because the alcohol level never overpowered the fruity flavors. Likewise, heavy-handed, smoky, oaky aromas that could have made it taste like "furniture" didn't bury the fruit. If it was a red wine, it wasn't too tannic, so the inside of your mouth and gums didn't feel like dried-out saddle leather. The wine didn't do any of these things, which means it was delicious and it was well balanced.

A wine's "finish" is the lingering taste it leaves behind in your mouth. The longer the finish, the higher the quality of the wine.

Of course, you can always flummox the snobs entirely by simply murmuring, "Delicious." In the end, that's all that counts, isn't it?

Wine
Service

Wine service covers a lot of ground, from the aesthetic to the practical to both (glassware has elements of beauty, as well as an effect on taste). It involves how wine is served in restaurants and at home—opening, aerating, decanting, and preserving a bottle of wine. There are gadgets galore that a wine enthusiast may want to collect, so I'll touch on them in this chapter, too. The main thing to keep in mind is that wine service should be servicing *you*, the wine lover!

Restaurant Service

Surely nothing is more annoying than spending considerable time and effort ordering a wine, only to have the server return to say, "I'm sorry, but we're out of that wine." Wine inventories do get depleted, but if such a mishap occurs, rather than burdening you with figuring out what to do next, the server should immediately say, "May I suggest instead _____?" indicating a similar style wine of comparable price. Some restaurants really put the customer back in customer service by offering a higher value wine at your original selection's price. These restaurants are to be treasured and rewarded with future business. If, after two tries of finding a wine that fits your style and pocketbook fails, ask to see the manager. Most often he or she will work it out.

When the server shows you the wine you presumably ordered, take a good look at the label. Is it in fact the right wine? You'd be amazed at how many wines are presented that are different from what was ordered. The most common mistake is in the vintage. Many restaurants, even the best ones, don't change their list when the vintage of a wine in their inventory changes. The wine server should mention the discrepancy and ask if you still want the wine. If the server does not mention the vintage change, be on the lookout for other unwanted variations. For instance, many producers have Cabernets or Chardonnays that are designated specifically Napa Valley (a premium location) versus plain old California (a less expensive blend of locations). Or a Cabernet may be a more expensive "reserve" or "proprietor's blend" instead of the winery's regular Cabernet. Each of these variations has a quality and price difference. Make sure that what's on the label is what you ordered. If the server has made the mistake of opening the wine before you've had an opportunity to examine the label and the opened wine is not what you ordered, don't hesitate to send it back. After all, if you ordered fish and were served a steak . . . you get the idea.

Sometimes the problem is the condition of the wine presented. Are there signs of maltreatment? If you see sticky wine residue, a stained label, or a protruding cork, it means the bottle may have been exposed to extreme heat. In the absence of obvious abuse, here's how to be a good wine welfare worker: When the server presents the wine for your inspection, put your hand on the bottle as you read. If the bottle is warm to your touch (warmer than room temperature) it may have been stored improperly and is a red flag that the wine may not be sound. (Those cute little out of the way restaurants with almost no storage space are often the biggest offenders.)

If you've ordered an expensive, older wine in a high-end restaurant, the wine should be presented in a wine "cradle" (an angled carrier), not upright. If the wine has left its storage rack and then been tilted upright, the sediment will have mixed with the contents, which means you should refuse the bottle and have the server bring you another. Take that wine lying down!

Opening Acts

Once you have accepted the bottle, the server will open it and pour a small amount in a glass for your further approval. If you have ordered a white wine with appetizers and a red for the entrée, ask to taste both when the wines are brought to you for confirmation. The red should be opened right away, aerated or decanted as needed, and be ready to serve when the main course arrives. If the restaurant is on the pretentious side—complete with a costumed sommelier sporting a tastevin swinging from a chain—the server may pour a bit into this silver cup and taste it. This ritual is merely a carryover from the old days, when poisoning persons of importance was all the rage and tasting food and wine was not foppery but a security issue. The server may also offer you the cork to sniff or lay it on the table next to you, which is a useless theatrical flourish. Hardly anyone can discern off odors or flavors from examining the cork, and in a moment you are going to get much better information by actually smelling and tasting the wine poured. My advice: Ignore the cork.

Before you taste the poured sample, swirl it around in the glass to aerate the wine. This will allow you to smell and taste with greater ease since aeration brings out the flavors (or defects) and you can make your judgment accordingly. In fact, you really don't need to taste the wine at all. If the wine is bad, your nose will tell you. So what are you looking for and what do you do about it?

It all comes down to deciding if the wine is sound or undrinkable. By sound I mean that it's not tainted or oxidized. Any of the following symptoms are cause for refusing the wine:

1. **Moldy, Musty Smell.** Five percent of wines are tainted from an infection in the cork. Refuse it, saying the wine is "corked."

2. **Flat, Lifeless.** Overheated in transport or storage, the wine has had its flavors cooked out. Just say it's "cooked."

3. **Rotten Eggs.** Hydrogen sulphide is present. It should have been left at the winery. Send it back.

4. **Sherry-like Odors.** Only Sherry should have the nutty flavor of Sherry. Regular wine with this aroma has been oxidized or "cooked." It doesn't belong on your table.

5. **Off Color.** Not to be confused with a dirty joke, off color means a white wine that is brownish in color or a red wine with a brown or yellow rim.

One thing you can safely ignore are tiny white crystals that appear like sand in white wine. These tartrate deposits, a residue of cold filtering, are harmless and tasteless. And if sediment or cork bits are present, they are also harmless but indicate a need for straining before being poured.

Tasting a poured sample is not like trying on shoes until you find a pair that you particularly like. You can't refuse a wine on subjective grounds. So if you just don't like what you're tasting, sip and bear it, making a mental note to avoid the wine next time. You may get lucky with an accommodating restaurant that permits this change of heart, using the wine you didn't like to cook with or to sell by the glass, but it's an exception, not the rule. If, however, the waiter has grossly misrepresented the wine's character, telling you for instance that sweet Sauternes is a dry white wine, then you are within your right to order a new bottle—and perhaps a new server.

Working with Your Server

After you've chosen your wine, make sure you seize the initiative and tell your server how you want it served. Servers like to refill glasses that are still half full so that the host will have to reorder faster, which increases the bill and the tip. Top gastronomic restaurants do not allow this. The sommelier teaches the servers that a glass should be poured one third full, not only because it allows for swirling, but because it's more aesthetically pleasing. So get into the habit of telling your waiter to fill the wine glasses only one third full and, more important, to ask each person at the table if they want wine before pouring or refilling their glass. The server doesn't need to interrupt the table conversation. Merely holding the bottle near the glass should provoke a yes or no signal from your guests. Reorders are, of course, the province of the host. The server might ask, "Would you like another bottle of the same or would you prefer a different wine?" If it appears that only one or two people at the table are short of wine, it's perfectly appropriate to shift to wine by the glass. The Wine Diva does not believe in wasting money or wine.

Playing TAG

The three ways to get the most out of a bottle of wine make for a nice snappy acronym: TAG for temperature, aeration, and glassware. I think this tip alone is worth the price of the book! If you remember nothing else about serving wine remember TAG, because these three steps can make a $10 wine taste like a $30 bottle.

Some Like It Hot, but Wines Do Not!

Temperature is the single most important factor in improving or detracting from your wine drinking pleasure. Yet both at home and in restaurants, we tend to pay less attention to this than we should. It's sad but true that every night, across the country, people are drinking white wines that are too cold and red wines that are too warm. The Wine Diva comes to the rescue with the following simple rules and repair methods.

White wines should be served cool, not cold (the temperature in your refrigerator is probably about 38 degrees Fahrenheit— great for beer, but too cold for white wine). At home take chilled whites out of the fridge ten minutes ahead of

Cool It!

Let's say you decide on a sultry summer evening, it's too hot to cook. You want to go out for dinner at your favorite little restaurant, which doesn't have a wine list. You can bring your own bottle, and tonight you know you'll want a nice chilled white wine. Just take out a Vacuvin Rapid Ice wine chiller sleeve, (available at fine wine stores, online at www.cooking.com, and at virtually all online wine accessory outfits) from your freezer and slip it over the bottle. In the twenty minutes it takes you to get to the restaurant the wine will be properly chilled and ready to pour just as you are being seated. Now that's refreshing!

A Chilling Experiment

I bought red, white, and sparkling wines and conducted the five chilling experiments below many times to compare results. Set your kitchen timer to the number of minutes I indicate to take the guesswork out of serving wine at the best temperature.

Salt water is the fastest way to cool your wines. Why? Because salt water lowers the freezing point of the ice, which allows the water to be colder. Water (salt or tap) also absorbs more heat from the wine than air can, which is why wine cools faster in water than it does in the freezer where cold air is used as the cooling mechanism.

(In physics terms, water has a "higher specific heat" content so it is able to absorb more heat than air can.)

To make salt water, just add a third to a half cup of salt to an ice bucket. At about a dollar for a box of salt, it doesn't cost much to do this. Or if you have brought your own wine to a restaurant, ask the waiter to bring one—or preferably two—salt shakers. Why bother? Because using tap water takes 50 percent more time to cool your wine than making salt water. Or said another way, using salt water instead of tap water in an ice bucket cuts the time by one third.

	Ice Bucket w/salt water	Ice Bucket w/tap water	Freezer	Fridge	Vacuvin Rapid Ice Gel Sleeve*
SPARKLING Cold to the Touch	20 min	30 min	40 min	90 min	
WHITE Very Cool to the Touch	10 min	15 min	20 min	45 min	15 min
RED Slightly Cool to the Touch	3 min	5 min	7 min	15 min	

*The packaging for the Vacuvin Rapid Ice gel sleeve says it can bring a room temperature white wine to proper serving temp in five minutes. It took only five to six minutes to bring a red to being slightly cool, but it took fifteen minutes to cool a white. I didn't even bother trying it with the sparkling. So I'd suggest this product for cooling a red wine quickly or carrying prechilled wines to another location, say to a picnic or someone's house for dinner.

time to let them get to pouring temperature, which is *cool* to the touch. If a white wine is brought to you at the restaurant cold and then placed in an ice bucket, go ahead and have an inch or two poured in everyone's glass, but then kick the bucket! Put the bottle on the table to warm up for ten minutes. By then you'll be ready for a refill.

Sparkling wines should be *cold* to the touch and therefore should be put in an ice bucket. The cold keeps the bubbles (CO_2) in the bubbly. Once the sparkler warms up, the bubbles disappear, and the delightful spritz goes away forever.

What if you have a white wine that's too warm? The Wine Diva has a foolproof, dazzlingly simple tip. When you are in a hurry to chill a wine, add about a third of a cup of salt to the ice bucket. Yes, you heard me right, salt. Using salt water in an ice bucket cuts the chilling time by one third—in the case of a bottle of white wine, from fifteen minutes to a mere ten. Why? Because salt causes ice to melt at a lower temperature than fresh water. So, whether you're at home or dining out, you can have a warm wine ready to drink just by pouring the salt shaker into the ice bucket.

I have had to ask for the salt shaker in many restaurants when friends bring a bottle and forget to chill the bottle of white wine first. Some waiters are either haughty or disbelieving when I ask for another salt shaker (so we keep ours to use at the table), but I stick to my guns because I know, and they don't. Other waiters are curious and want to learn a new trick. So no matter if they are disbelievers or curious, here's what I do: I ask for an empty glass and offer the server a small taste of the wine that chilled in salt water in just ten minutes. The doubters turn into believers.

It may surprise you when I say red wines should be just slightly cool to the touch when they come to the table. People often confuse serving or cellar temperature with room temperature. When room temperature meant the chilly château's 60 to 65 degrees Fahrenheit, cool by today's standards, it was fine as a serving temperature. But today if you don't have a temperature-controlled wine cellar, chances are your wine's been stored in a room with a temperature more like 70 to 75 degrees. If your red wine is that warm, give it a cold bath. Submerge the bottle in an ice bucket up to its neck for five minutes. This chilling experience will revive the wine to cellar temperature for a better taste experience.

Aeration: It's All in the Timing

Mixing air with wine just before pouring is one of the easiest ways to improve its taste. I can see your thought balloon: "Wait! You said that air is the enemy of wine, and now you're telling me to mix air and wine?" Precisely. It's all in the timing. Exposure to air while wine is in storage and supposed to be resting speeds up the aging process, sometimes to the point of destroying the flavors or the wine's drinkability. Think of wine in the bottle as being in hibernation. Once it's open, it wants big gulps of air, to breathe until it comes fully alive. When wine is ready to wake up, mixing air and wine actually does something beautiful. Young red wines pulled from your cellar benefit from a little time in a decanter to allow the flavors to come forth. Also, red wines are full of tannins, the same substance found in tea. Tannins are a vital element of these powerful wines, giving them the backbone to age gracefully. But tannins may give a bitter taste or rough, dried-out feeling in the mouth (I call it "the Harris Tweed" effect) while you're drinking the wine. Tea drinkers often tame the tannin in tea by adding milk. Aeration tames the tannins in red wines to a silky, soft, more pleasant feeling in the mouth.

Full-bodied red wines such as Cabernet, Bordeaux, Syrah, or Barolo that are under five years old can take an hour's "instant aging" in a decanter. Older wines require less since they are already at or approaching maturity. I recommend decanting these older wines no more than ten minutes prior to serving just to get the mustiness out. Very old wines (twenty years or more) should be opened and poured after only two or three minutes since their flavors and aromas are fragile.

So how do you aerate wines? There are two ways to mix air and wine: In a glass or in a decanter. In a glass, fill the bowl no more than one third full, swirl the wine around a few turns, and that's it.

Aerating wine in a decanter achieves the same end as in a glass but because the surface of a decanter is greater, less swirling is required. Simply pouring the wine from bottle to decanter infuses air, but the best decanters have wide mouths and especially broad bottoms so that more surface area of the wine is exposed to air. You don't need a special wine decanter to get the desired effect. A glass juice pitcher or, in a pinch, even a flower vase (cleaned and rinsed with hot water so no soap residue remains) will do just fine.

Decanting wines, particularly older red wines, provides two benefits—aeration, which softens the wine, and sediment separation, which clarifies it.

An older red wine needs to have the sediment that accumulated during aging separated from the clear wine on top. If you are at home, select your wine a day in advance, then stand it up until decanting. This will allow the sediment to settle in the bottom of the bottle for easier separation at decanting time.

If you've forgotten to stand your wine upright ahead of time, you can clarify it by carefully pouring into a decanter while holding the bottle on its side (or nearly so). As you pour, watch the wine flowing from the bottle. Having a light source (window, lamp, flashlight, candle, etc.) behind the bottle and decanter is helpful. As soon as the decanted wine begins to look cloudy or chunks of sludge appear, stop pouring! The appearance of this stuff means that sediment is creeping into the clear wine. Trust me. You don't want to drink these bitter dregs. The loss of useable wine in this controlled pour is almost always minimal, no more than an ounce or two.

Instead of treating young tannic red wine with kid gloves, use tough love to aerate it quickly: Toss the wine back and forth between two decanters, two orange juice pitchers, or two flower vases. Just toss and taste till you feel the wine has the soft mouth feel you like!

It's fun to do a simple test of the results of aeration and decanting. Assuming that you are not having a '61 Lafite for dinner, pour half of the wine you are going to have into a decanter an hour before serving. Keep the remainder in the open bottle and pour both at serving time. I have performed this experiment many times at tastings without the participants knowing that both glasses are in fact the same wine, just opened an hour apart. Participants almost always insist that the wine opened earlier is far superior! And when I trick them by comparing a decanted Cab at room temperature with one decanted but slightly cool, they insist that the latter is a different and better wine.

If you're at a restaurant don't be embarrassed to ask for a decanter, especially if you are having a big red. The waiter shouldn't balk at this "extra" service, for it's no more than asking him to make another trip for a spoon to help twirl your pasta or for mustard in addition to the catsup. If the restaurant has no decanter—restaurants with wines on their list costing $60 and up without decanters ought to be ashamed of themselves— ask for the kind of pitcher they use for Bloody Marys or iced tea. I once ordered an expensive Barolo that without question needed the benefit of aerating/ decanting. The waiter insisted that the wine didn't need decanting, an error not only in fact but in customer service. The truth was that they didn't have a decanter. I shamed the server and his bartender accomplice by requesting and using a perfectly good glass water pitcher. It worked fine, the wine was delicious, and my hope is that the server learned a lesson.

Decanters: Divine or Down to Earth

If you serve old red wines regularly, a decanter is a must. Aerating and clarifying old red wines in a decanter is so much easier and produces a better result than doing it any other way. Decanters come at many price points in many styles. You can buy them at Pottery Barn, Bed Bath & Beyond, and Crate & Barrel, and they'll only set you back $10 to $20. Or splurge on truly exquisite Waterford costing $50 to $300, or Baccarat at $460 to $1,300. Or you can use the pitcher that came as a premium with six cans of orange juice. They'll all do the job. The only essential requirement of a decanter is that it be made from glass or crystal, not metal or plastic, to prevent the container containing the wine's flavor.

Great Glassware

You may order a beer in a pewter mug or a coffee in a china cup, but wine is always served in a glass. Partly custom and elegance on the dinner table, there are some practical reasons as well. The size, shape, and type of glass all contribute to how a wine tastes.

Size

In football players and wineglasses, large is better than small. Large glasses, filled no more than one third full, allow you to swirl wine vigorously, aerating it without spilling it all over your clothes. Partially filled wineglasses also look better at the table, at least to my eye. If you are at a restaurant where a wine by the glass turns out to be filled to the brim, ask for a second glass and divide and conquer. The act of dividing will make the wine happy because it will allow more aeration—not to mention the opportunity to share with a table companion if you're feeling generous.

Shape

Each color of wine has a specific shaped glass. Red wines are usually served in one of two shaped glasses—big, round-bowled Burgundy glasses, sometimes called balloons, or large, tall, tulip-shaped Bordeaux style glasses. The universal wineglass, for serving both red and white wine, is somewhere in the middle of these two shapes. If you have little storage space, are on a budget, or like to host lots of wine tastings, universal glasses are convenient. White wines don't emit as many flavors in swirling and aerating as reds, so the glasses for whites are usually smaller and shorter. But all wines benefit from swirling, so make sure you have big enough glasses. The difference in shape for reds and whites makes for a prettier table setting, as well as giving the server—you or the waiter—a clue as to which wine goes into which glass. Sherries and ports are served in smaller versions of the tulip shape called *copitas*.

Sparkling wines need to be served in a flute, a tall, narrow glass that minimizes the surface of the wine exposed to warm air and therefore keeps the wine cooler and bubble loss to a minimum. If anyone you know attempts to serve you Champagne in a glass that looks like a shallow saucer, called a *coupe*, call the wine police. These wide-mouthed glasses let the bubbles dissipate quickly, so the wine can go flat. Use them instead for ice cream or sorbet. And if you wonder how the custom of serving Champagne in inappropriately wide-mouthed glasses began, read the sidebar below.

Type

Wineglasses can mean plain glass or crystal. Avoid colored glass so that you can enjoy the color of the wine and be able to see if the wine is cloudy, which could mean the wine may have problems. Crystal is not only more elegant in appearance, it functions differently. Unlike plain glass, which has a very smooth surface, crystal is microscopically rough. While you may not detect this roughness, the

Oh My, Marie!

If those very shallow, wide, *coupe* Champagne glasses remind you of a certain part of a woman's anatomy, you're more on target than you might have known. Legend has it that they were first modeled after the breasts of Marie-Antoinette, the wife of French King Louis XVI. Even more intriguing is the wine lore that Marie herself had casts taken of her breasts in order to make special porcelain drinking vessels. Apparently, she wanted her courtiers to drink to her health from them—more appealing than drinking out of a glass slipper, I suppose.

wine does; and for the wine, it's all pleasure. Just as a rough loofah sponge feels great on your back in the shower, wine says "ahhh" by releasing more aromatic flavor than it would in a smooth-surfaced glass. Crystal glasses usually have thinner walls than less expensive glass, too, another big plus. The alcohol in the wine evaporates more rapidly in a thin-walled glass, so the wine doesn't taste "hot" in the back of your mouth. When you swirl off the blanket of alcohol lying on the wine's surface the aromas are released into your awaiting nose faster. Thin crystal is also more helpful if you need to warm your too-chilled white wine. By cupping the glass in your hand, your body warmth warms the wine. So, unless you are deliberately warming a wine that's too cold, hold your glass by the stem.

The Gift of Glass

When it comes to gift giving, I prefer to give wineglasses more than a bottle of wine. They give the recipients years of increased drinking pleasure, which is why I call them "the gift that keeps on giving." Before you start giving them away, be sure you gift yourself! They come in price points to fit all wallets. Some of the most popular brands and prices of crystal stemware include:

BRAND	PRICE PER RED BORDEAUX GLASS
Spiegelau "Vino Grande" series	$7
Spiegelau "Authentis" series	$9
Ravenscroft "Sommelier"	$13
Riedel "Vinum"	$18

Crystal Clear Care

We all know crystal is fragile and should be handled with care. But did you know that the stem is connected to the bowl of the glass by a small patch of molten glass? Called a "stuck" stem, this patch is a weak point, so holding the stem while drying the bowl can result in twisting the whole thing apart. Hold the bowl of the glass under the towel while drying. I use disposable paper coffee filters for drying because they don't leave loose fibers, are absorbent, and are inexpensive.

Soap residue is the other thing to avoid. While most modern dishwashers do a pretty good job of cleaning, some don't do as well in rinsing. You may want to add a rinsing agent (available in most supermarkets) to your dishwasher when doing your crystal. Wineries use dishwashers for their tasting room glasses, but most, if not all, run them on very hot water without soap. I like to do my crystal by hand using very little soap, a sponge separate from the one I use to wipe down countertops or clean off plates, and hot water.

Tools and Toys

Wine paraphernalia, from corkscrews to foil cutters, is a cottage industry. While some of it is quite useful, the rest is in the "Dad's Christmas tie" category. Still, the proper gear greatly increases the pleasure of drinking wine, whether in public or private. Most of the many available wine gadgets can be seen by visiting my favorite wine accessories Web site, winestuff.com.

Openers and Closures

Opening a wine bottle can be easy or hard, depending on the tool you use. Screw caps need only a flick of your wrist, and are becoming more and more common (see pages 19–20). But as long as there are corks, you need tools. Naturally there have been any number of corkscrews, pullers, and pop-ups designed and used since the beginning of bottled wine. Here are some of the most common variations:

1. **The Waiter's Corkscrew.** Folded, it's easily carried in a pocket. Opened into the butterfly position it will open almost any bottle, although some practice is required. I suggest you save this for travel or picnics. There are easier ways to get at your wine.

2. **The Winged Screw.** Turn the screw into the cork and when the wings fly up, push them down to lever the cork out. Easier than the waiter's version, but still requires some skill.

3. **"Ah-so."** This unusual opener is a favorite with tasting rooms and some bars because it removes the cork without putting a hole in it and can keep an older, more fragile cork intact. Instead you slide the shim blades of the opener between the cork and glass. Once you have worked the blades all the way down, pull straight up, and the cork comes out with the blades.

4. **The Screw Pull and the Rabbit.** These are for heavy users. Clamp the bottle top in the vise grips, lever up on the handle, and out pops the cork. Reverse the lever and the cork is freed. It's simple and fast. If you open a lot of bottles, this is the industrial assembly line opener.

5. **Cork Pop.** This is the easiest of all. Insert the needle through the cork, lightly press the button on the top once, and in one second, voilà—the cork is out! It's almost foolproof, and works well with the new synthetic corks. Its only drawback is that it's not recommended for magnums or other large sizes.

Every wine lover has an opening crisis at least once in a while. What to do if you can't open your wine? Put the bottle's neck under hot running water for five to ten seconds. That quick exposure to heat makes the glass expand temporarily just enough so the cork slithers out without protest.

Champagne needs no special tools for opening. You're on your own. First, remove the foil, then point the bottle in a safe direction, undoing the wire that holds the cork in place. Still pointing the top of the bottle away from you, carefully twist the cork in one direction and the bottle in another until it loosens and comes out with a soft sigh. Dramatic as it may be, a loud pop can spill out the precious wine. I suggest putting a bar towel over the cork as you twist so that neither cork nor Champagne goes flying. (I hereby exempt World Series champions in locker rooms from this rule.) I know another method for opening a Champagne bottle, but do not try this at home! Made popular by Napoleon's cavalry officers, it involves sabering the top off with one well-placed slash. If you attend one of the corporate or charity events where I speak, you will see me perform it as a theatrical finale.

Other Accessories

One gadget I find essential is a **foil cutter**, which removes the metal foil on top before you use a corkscrew. If you habitually put a corkscrew through the lead foil, the screw tip will become dull and wind up not doing its job as well. The foil cutter is safe, inexpensive, and works great.

Funnels are nice to own if you ever serve big wines that may have some serious sediment. In addition to straining sediment out, funnels usually have small holes in the spout to aerate wine as it's poured through. Very few people have funnels, so keep them in mind when you need a gift for those who can afford older, more expensive wines. Maybe you'll be invited to share those great wines more often.

Finally, cellar **thermometers** can be a good investment. The point is to monitor whether or not your wines have suffered any potentially adverse temperatures, not to note the current conditions. Cellar thermometers can alert you to a problem early on, so you can nip it in the bud. It's like a wine smoke detector. So, I recommend the minimum-maximum type, which simply tells you how hot or cold the cellar has been since you last set the thermometer.

Stain Removers

It's the bane of any self-respecting host or hostess: Red wine stains on their brilliant white tablecloth or beige Berber rug. Happily, a product that works wonders, called Wine Away, is available from www.evergreenlabs.com, most wine accessories Web sites, and many housewares stores. Use a cloth or paper towel to blot, not wipe up the excess spilled wine; then douse the area with the stain remover. Wait a minute or two and blot again with a clean paper towel. Magically, the stain will be gone. If you are without Wine Away, there are three ways to remove red wine stains using what you have on hand, though I can't promise the same magic.

1. Squeeze a mixture of lemon juice and water onto the stain and blot dry.

2. Dab a mixture of white wine or cider vinegar and water onto the stain. Blot and dry.

3. Do the same as above using an unoaked white wine such as Sauvignon Blanc, Pinot Grigio, Muscadet, or Chablis with high acidity. (Do not use Chardonnay; it doesn't have enough acid.)

Preserving Your Wine

Unless you have a rather large wine-drinking family, you will not finish every bottle of wine you open in one evening. But leftover wine is far from leftover food you can just toss in a plastic container, put in the back of the fridge, and promptly forget about. For one thing, how could you ever forget you have wine? More important, wines that are simply recorked only last a day or two, which means you are wasting most of your $10 to $15 bottle of wine over and over and over again throughout the year. Unless, that is, you don't leave it to its own devices, but do use these devices.

For about the cost of a bottle of wine you can buy a Vacuvin vacuum wine saver, a hand-operated pump that sucks the air out of the bottle. Also available for about the same price is an aerosol, Private Preserve Wine Preserver, that spreads a nitrogen-based inert gas like a blanket over the surface of the leftover wine to seal out air for about four days. You just spray a few squirts into the bottle and recork. One can preserve about 120 bottles, which comes out to about 8 cents per bottle of wine. The Pek Wine Steward, a metal cone into which a wine bottle is inserted, automatically injects a more expensive and effective inert gas, argon, into the bottle. While the metal cone costs $99, the gas cartridges sell separately for $12 for a pack of four. Each cartridge can preserve 10 bottles of wine, which translates to 30 cents a bottle—but saves wine for a week. My personal favorite—and the least expensive—way to preserve any leftover wine is to pour it into a clean, empty Perrier bottle with a screw cap, or a Grolsch beer bottle, which has a metal flip top stopper. It's pure logic: Beer, sparkling water, and soft drink manufacturers have to be certain that when customers reopen their products days later, they are going to taste fresh. So screw caps and metal stoppers must be airtight. Start saving those Perrier and Grolsch bottles and your wine will thank you.

A piece of seventeenth-century technology like a cork seems downright inadequate now, doesn't it? So think of recorking as a last option. If you do opt to simply put the cork back in, put the dry (top) end in first. It will be easier than using the other end, swollen by the wine. The seal won't be airtight because the cork has holes, including the large one you put in by opening the bottle. That's why rubber or plastic stoppers are better. They come in so many colorful, amusing varieties these days, it's fun to have several on hand.

You can buy preservation devices for Champagne, but save your money. Here's why: What happens when you open a soft drink in a metal can, can't finish it, and put it back in the fridge? It still has its sparkle when you drink it the next day. The same thing goes for Champagne. The reason that soft drinks and Champagne can keep their effervescence for a day in an open container in the fridge is that the CO_2 in these beverages is heavier than air and provides a "blanket" over their surfaces. So from now on just stick the bubbly back in the fridge and use the leftover for mimosas at breakfast or have it with lunch. Someone once said, "A meal without wine is called breakfast," but in this case a breakfast with wine is divine.

A Final Thought

Wine service is like other forms of etiquette: Its purpose is not to make life difficult or complicated but to make it run smoothly and more enjoyably. If you don't want to worry about the ins and outs of serving wine, just raise your glass and sip slowly. I hope you'll get more pleasure from wine drinking by following these tips, but the key word is *enjoy*.

Wine
at *Home*

If you are a regular wine drinker, you consume far more wine at home than you do in restaurants. Almost everyone starts with selecting the food menu and then figuring out what wines to serve. Once you read my WHITE CUFFS roadmap on how to pair food and wine (pages 48–55), you'll be able to do that as easily as pulling a cork with one white-cuffed hand tied behind your back. If you have taken my advice on stocking wine (pages 15–43), you'll have wines of varying colors, weights, and cost at your disposal in your "cellar" (whether under the bed or in a wine cooler). So what else do you need to know?

Think about your dining habits. You probably eat at home with your family for most of your meals, dine out casually or order in for others. Occasionally, you either entertain at home or dress up for a big night out at a white tablecloth restaurant. Special occasions are special, so you plan for them separately. I like having a general game plan ahead of time, so I have a little cheat sheet for choosing wine in each of these situations. Do make up your own chart—and keep adjusting it. In addition to the usual wines you enjoy (Sauvignon Blanc, Pinot Grigio,

**Match the weight of the wine to
the weight of the food you are serving**

Casual Family Meals

Whites

Light-bodied: Sauvignon Blanc/Sancerre, Riesling, Pinot Blanc,
Chablis, Muscadet, Pinot Grigio, Orvieto, Soave, Vermentino, Verdicchio

Medium-bodied: Fumé Blanc, Chenin Blanc, Pinot Gris, white
Burgundy, white Bordeaux, Greco, Fiano, Gavi, Arneis, Falanghina, Albariño,
Rueda

Full-bodied: Chardonnay, Viognier

Weekends, Dinner Parties, and Special Occasions

Whites

Light-bodied: Chablis, Premier and Grand Crus, Riesling

Medium-bodied: white Burgundy, white Bordeaux, Pouilly-Fumé,
Vouvray, Pinot Gris, Gewürztraminer, Grüner Veltliner

Full-bodied: Chardonnay, Chardonnay/Semillon blend,
Viognier/Condrieu, white Burgundy, white Rhône blend

Big Occasions

Whites

Light-bodied: Riesling

Medium-bodied: white Burgundy, white Bordeaux

Full-bodied: Chardonnay, white Burgundy, Condrieu

$10–20 a bottle

Reds

Light-bodied: Beaujolais-Villages, Bourgeuil, Chinon, Rioja-Crianza, Chianti, Valpolicella, Bardolino, Barbera

Medium-bodied: Merlot, Pinot Noir, red Burgundy, red Bordeaux, Côtes du Rhône, Cru Beaujolais, Dolcetto, Sangiovese, Barbera

Full-bodied: Merlot, Cabernet, Zinfandel, Syrah/Shiraz, Malbec

Sparkling

Light-bodied: Prosecco, Cava, Cremant d'Loire

Light- and medium-bodied: Sparkling wine

$25–50 a bottle

Reds

Medium-bodied: Pinot Noir, Merlot, Cabernet, red Burgundy, red Bordeaux "Cru Bourgeois," Crozes-Hermitage, Cornas, St-Joseph, St-Emilion "satellites" and Lalande-de-Pomerol, Chianti Classico, Chianti Classico Riserva, Rioja Riserva, Rioja Gran Riserva

Full-bodied: Merlot, Cabernet, Zinfandel, Syrah/Shiraz, Châteauneuf-du-Pape

Sparkling

Light-, medium-, and full-bodied: non-vintage Champagne, sparkling wines

$75 and up

Reds

Medium-bodied: Pinot Noir, red Burgundy "Grand Cru"

Full-bodied: Merlot, Cabernet, Syrah/Shiraz, 61 Great Château wines, St-Emilion and Pomerol, Châteauneuf-du-Pape, Hermitage, Côte-Rotie, Barolo, Barbaresco, Brunello di Montalcino, Super Tuscans, Amarone, Taurasi

Sparkling

Full-bodied: vintage Champagne

Chardonnay, Pinot Noir, Merlot, and Cabernet), I'd love you to try these delicious alternatives. I've indicated if they are light- (L), medium- (M), or full- (F) bodied so you can easily pair them with delicate, medium, or heavy dishes.

Use your own customized chart as a reminder that each time you dine is a new opportunity to expand your wine horizons. Another important point about choosing wines for different occasions: Don't neglect that jewel in your "cellar" until it's past its prime. Too many people tell me they don't believe a significant enough time has arrived to open a prized wine. I say, "Nonsense!" Keep your eye on this special bottle of wine and create an event for it. Celebrate the first day of spring or make up a family holiday—National Kazoo Day or No News Is Good News Day. Because my philosophy is "If not now, when?" and "If not us, who?"

When you do decide to serve a wine a cut above your everyday choices, you'll be planning a menu based on the wine rather than vice versa. I do this when I've decided to serve one of my treasures—an old Barolo, for instance. I want my guests to get the utmost pleasure from this great wine, so I make simple food as a quiet chorus backing up the star of the evening.

Surround the star with lesser wines served with other courses so that the experience of tasting one great wine isn't diluted by two or three other high-voltage costars. Serving only one of your special wines at a meal not only lets you focus on it better, it means you can look forward to another occasion with its own star. If possible, let the star make its grand entrance toward the end of the meal after your lesser wines have appeared.

Parties at Home

Serving old-fashioneds at cocktail parties is about as old-fashioned as calling them cocktail parties in the first place. Wine rather than mixed drinks is the beverage of choice at most gatherings these days—with the possible exception of summer cookouts, where beer still rules.

For your wine parties, I recommend you buy big bottles—1.5 liters (equivalent to two regular bottles, called magnums). Larger bottles are, ounce for ounce, cheaper than the regular size, and they are more convenient to serve because you don't have to open or store as many bottles. While many 1.5 liter bottles are at the low end of the quality and price spectrum (around $12 to $14 a bottle), a small step up in price (to $19 to $20) pays big quality dividends. In colder weather, figure most of your guests will drink more red than white wine and on average each wine drinker will drink a quarter of a big bottle (half of a regular size bottle) over the course of the party. (This is based on consumption of three four-ounce glasses per person over a three-hour period in which food is served.) So if you are having forty for cocktails you need five big bottles (three red and two white) or ten regular bottles (six red and four white). In warmer weather the reverse will be true and you should order more white than red. If you are serving only Champagne or sparkling wine, one bottle serves five glasses, so you'll need one case of bubbly to pour sixty glasses. I always like having backups of similar wines in regular-size bottles in case my guests are thirstier than usual. If I don't need to open extra bottles at the party, I can always use them for family meals. Even wine that's been chilled can be put back in your wine

rack or under the bed without harm, safe and
sound for your next soiree.

Yes, in My Backyard: Storing Wine for Parties

A common, if infrequent, Wine Diva dilemma is
where oh where to put those cases before the
party. And at holiday time there is often a lot of
jockeying for space in the fridge and complaints
about "all that wine taking up space I need for the
turkey." It's a matter of thinking outside the box.
Or in this case, outside the case.

Use your own backyard as long as it's not
freezing or sweltering. If you own a car, use the
trunk. If you're a city dweller, use the balcony or
fire escape, or say a friendly hello to your
neighbors, ask to borrow their space, and then
give them a bottle as a thank-you. If none of these
options is available, your regular wine merchant
(whom you have cultivated, as I suggested on page
23) may store your wines for up to a week and
then deliver them the day of your party. For any
outdoor options, pay attention to the weather,
because very hot temperatures will "cook" the
taste right out of your wines, and if the
temperature dips below freezing, your bottles
could explode, resulting in wine slush—a terrible
end for a perfectly innocent grape.

Wine and Special Occasions

From annual holidays such as Thanksgiving,
Chanukah, and New Year's Eve to once in a lifetime
milestones like your thirtieth wedding anniversary,
retirement, or a bar mitzvah, special moments
become all the more special when wine is served.
But what is the *right* wine for each occasion? It
might be your most prized vintage bottle or simply
the best of your favorite producer. If it's special to

you, your enthusiasm will be contagious, and your family and guests will feel extra appreciated: an unbroken circle of celebration.

The Holidays

When occasions have specific menus associated with them—turkey on Thanksgiving, ham at Easter—you may be tempted to take the easy way out and serve the same wines year after year. That's fine, I suppose, if your picks got rave reviews. But you and your guests might suffer from wine burnout eventually. Why not enliven those holidays by trying new wines? Here are some of my favorites to tempt you to experiment:

Christmas

Cabernet would probably be your usual choice if you serve the traditional roast beef and Yorkshire pudding. To extend the Olde English theme, try claret, the English term for a red wine from Bordeaux. Then continue with Port for a dessert of pudding or trifle.

Thanksgiving

I remember I used to host Thanksgiving dinner for all of my single friends who had nowhere else to be (the orphans' dinner, I called it). I would ask them to suggest or bring their favorite side dish, the one that Mom used to

Clarifying Claret

The English have been world-class wine drinkers for a long time. They popularized Port from Oporto in Portugal, Sherry from Jerez in Spain, and became fond of red wines from Bordeaux in the fourteenth century. English wine merchants originally bought fresh, light-colored (*clairet* in French) red wine in barrels then transported it by ship to England for bottling. These wines had to be consumed within a year at most. By the second half of the seventeenth century, however, a new style of Bordeaux emerged. These wines were higher quality, lasted many years, and were deeper color. Despite the style change, the name for the wines persisted. It was only a matter of time until the French adjective *clairet* morphed into the English noun claret despite the darker color of the wine.

make—creamed onions, caramelized yams with the sticky white stuff on top, stuffing with sausage and sage, cranberry sauce with nuts and oranges. It was a festive, albeit eclectic, feast. As I was still in my pre-Diva stage, I did not even consider what wines would go with this mélange. But today I love to at least try.

Thanksgiving can be as tough as overcooked turkey in terms of wine pairing—and it's not the turkey's fault. Turkey is lean and therefore pretty bland, but those infamous side dishes with a multitude of flavors are a challenge. If your budget can take it, Champagne is a great Thanksgiving wine. It cuts through the grease on the turkey skin, knocks down the overpowering fruit of the sweeter sides, and sparks up the gravy-covered mashed potatoes. I also like to try out inexpensive wines, bubblies at $10 to $12 a bottle, and oh-so-quaffable Beaujolais Nouveau at around $7 a bottle. The release of the new vintage is usually timed to Thanksgiving, so I'm surely not the only one who's thought of this. This fresh wine is a very good choice, not only for food reasons, but for easing the strain on your pocketbook as you begin the holiday season. A higher quality Beaujolais, called Beaujolais-Villages, can be had for about $10. If you're having a crowd for Thanksgiving and want to spend about $10 to $15 a bottle, then I suggest my favorite all-purpose white wine, Riesling (from the Alsace region of France), or fruity reds like Pinot Noir, Australian Shiraz, or California Zinfandel, all of which can tackle the spicy, salty, smoky, or sweetish side dish flavors. I don't recommend the big reds—Cabernets, Syrahs, and Barolos—which are better for hearty red meats, not turkey and its accompaniments.

Easter

The traditional Easter ham is fairly salty and needs a wine to overcome the taste-deadening effect of this dish and to clear the palate for the next bite of food. As always, Champagne or another sparkling wine rises to this wine occasion. If you're a red wine fan, Pinot Noir and Merlot are great, but don't ignore Beaujolais cru (top tier Beaujolais named after ten specific villages). If Madonna can serve a Beaujolais cru called "Fleurie" at her wedding, you can certainly serve it for Easter dinner! And cru Beaujolais only runs about $15 a bottle. For those who prefer white, wines with a bit of sweetness are the best candidates to complement a ham's brown sugar glaze. So reach for a German Riesling—Kabinett (drier) or Spätlese (sweeter)—or a Chenin Blanc from California, called Vouvray in France's Loire Valley. And I can't forget our old faithful Chardonnay. Heavily oaked versions that are more akin to buttered popcorn or a butterscotch sundae will overpower the ham and clash with its saltiness. While this style is wonderful with other dishes, more and more often you can find a relatively new style Chardonnay on the scene: lighter, fruitier, more refreshing, and little or no oak. So have this underoaked understudy appear at your Easter performance. If you serve a lamb or beef roast for Easter dinner, then up the weight of the wine and serve red Bordeaux, Barolo, Brunello, or your favorite Merlot or Cabernet.

Jewish Holidays

How are kosher wines different from traditional wines? Kosher wines have nothing to do with the grape varieties, sweetness level, or type of wine, but rather how the wine is made. Kosher wines are produced in adherence to a strict set of

Out of the "Woods"

 Here's a list of lightly oaked Chardonnay from recent vintages to fit every budget, starting with the lowest priced:

- Calera "El Nino," $10.50
- Stag's Leap "Hawk Crest," $11
- Kali Heart Vineyards, $14
- Eden Vineyards "Wolff Vineyard," $17
- Rutherford Hill, $18
- Gallo of Sonoma "Two Rock Vineyard," $24
- Stony Hill, $27
- Trefethen "Estate," $28
- Grgich, $34
- Tablas Creek "Antithesis," $35
- Eden Vineyards Estate Bottled, $35
- Stag's Leap "Arcadia," $45
- Sonoma Coast Vineyards, $45
- Phelps "Ovation," $48
- HdV, $55
- Kistler "Vine Hill," $65

Some wine producers are going even further and making Chardonnay without any oak influence, which would have been unthinkable a few years ago! This new, crisp, refreshing style has been dubbed "naked Chardonnay." If you become a fan of these wines, as I have, the next list is a good starting point to try naked Chardonnay.

California:
- Martin & Weyrich "Huerhuero Creek," $9
- Four Vines Naked Chardonnay, $14
- Roshambo Winery "Imago," $18
- Morgan Winery "Mettalico," $20
- Michel Laroche at Rutherford Hill, $28
- Mayo Family "Laurel Hill Vineyard," $25
- Melville Vineyards "Inox," $30

Oregon:
- Rex Hill, $16
- Chehalen "Inox," $17
- Domaine Drouhin "Arthur," $27
- Argyle "Nuthouse," $28

Australia:
- The Wishing Tree, $9
- Yalumba "Y Series," $11
- Elderton, $14
- Mad Fish, $15
- Omrah $16
- Salitage, $29

New Zealand:
- Brancott Vineyards, $11
- Villa Maria "Private Bin," $13.50
- Kim Crawford, $17

guidelines laid out by rabbinical law in order to make them acceptable for consumption by religious Jews. For example, only Sabbath-observant, strictly Orthodox Jews are allowed to be involved from the vineyard to bottling.

In order for non-Jewish people to handle the wine at a restaurant and for it to remain kosher, kosher wines are boiled (flash pasteurized) for one to two seconds. Unfortunately, the wine loses some of its flavor from the heating. This type of kosher wine is referred to as *mevushal*.

Fortunately, the number of kosher wines has become much more extensive than the days when your only choice was a sweet, red Manischewitz, which was essentially sweetened Concord grape juice—as in plain old table grapes. If you're sentimental, you may still prefer it, but the variety of wines on the shelves today is absolutely amazing: Chardonnay, Pinot Grigio, Riesling, Chenin Blanc, and Viognier for whites; sparkling wines and even Champagne; and Cabernet, Merlot, Pinot Noir, Syrah, Zinfandel, Barbera, Sangiovese, and Pinotage for reds.

You can find great kosher wine from Bordeaux (Chateau Devise d'Ardilley) and, of course, Israel (Golan Heights Winery and Yarden Vineyards). Here in the United States, Baron Herzog, Royal Kedem, Hagafen Cellars, and Pine Ridge wines are consistently good from year to year. And let's not forget Australia's Teal Lake and South Africa's Backsberg Estate.

There is even kosher Champagne! Laurent Perrier and Nicholas Feuillatte make limited runs of kosher non-vintage brut Champagne.

Food and Wine Pairing for the Jewish Holidays

If you have read the Food and Wine Pairing chapter, you have an easy method for picking the best wine partners for your favorite traditional recipes. Here are four holiday dishes to show you how simple it is to use my "White Cuffs" approach.

	Oven Braised Brisket with Onions and Tomatoes
Weight of food?	Heavy, so dish needs full-bodied wines. Remember, you can be color-blind and choose from red or white wines.
Cooking method?	Slow braising turns meat brown, which points to use of an oaked wine.
Umami present?	Umami is present in slow-cooked meats AND in tomatoes, so avoid tannic reds like Cabernet, Syrah, and Zinfandel, as well as oaky Chardonnay (tannins leach into wine from the oak barrels). Instead pair foods containing umami with wines that are less tannic, like Pinot Noir, red Burgundy, Barbera, Merlot, and Shiraz. If you prefer white, try lightly oaked Chardonnays (see page 148) and white Burgundy and Bordeaux.
Fat in meat/fish?	No, brisket is lean meat, which needs a fruitier wine like Pinot Noir, Barbera, Merlot, and Shiraz or lightly oaked Chardonnay, which lets the fruit shine through. (Notice these are the same wines recommended for heavy, umami-filled dishes.) The fruitiness of these wines makes up for the lack of richness when there is precious little fat in the meat.
Fatty ingredients?	No
S Factor?	No spicy, salty, smoky ingredients to steer wine choice another way
	Layered Vegetable Kugel Casserole with Broccoli, Carrots, and Cauliflower
Weight of food?	Medium, so wines should be medium-bodied.
Cooking method?	Baking turns the kugel brown on top, which means oaked white or red wines. Whites include Chardonnay and white Burgundy and Bordeaux. Medium-bodied red selections include Pinot Noir, Shiraz, and Sangiovese-based Tuscan reds.
Umami in dish?	No
Fat in meat/fish?	Not applicable
Fatty ingredients?	No
S Factor?	No

Steamed Halibut in Borscht with Warm Cilantro, Ginger, and Horseradish Sauce

Weight of food?	Medium weight dish needs medium weight wines
Cooking method?	Steaming foods in water adds no flavor to the dish so use an unoaked white or very lightly oaked red. Medium-bodied whites include Albariño, Chenin Blanc, Grüner Veltliner, unoaked and lightly oaked Chardonnay (see page 148), as well as some white Burgundy and Bordeaux. Medium-bodied red wines include Pinot Noir, red Burgundy, Merlot, Shiraz, or Sangiovese-based reds from Tuscany.
Umami in dish?	No
Fat in meat/fish?	No
Fatty ingredients?	No
S Faotor?	Yes, the sauce contains horseradish, ginger, and cilantro, which means you need fruity wines with refreshing acidity to offset their spiciness. So play it again, Sam! The same wines I recommended above due to the cooking method are the best wine choices if the S Factor is in your dish.

Potato or Vegetable Latkes

Weight of food?	Light, so wine should be light-bodied.
Cooking method?	Frying in oil means you should use an unoaked white wine like a Sauvignon Blanc, Pinot Grigio, Chablis, Riesling, or a refreshing non-vintage Champagne or bubbly, which cuts through the oil.
Umami in dish?	No
Fat in meatfish?	Not applicable
Fatty ingredients?	If you like a big dollop of sour cream on top, then this prominent ingredient changes the equation and Chardonnay, with its affinity for cream, butter, and sour cream, would be the best partner.
S Factor?	No

Valentine's Day and New Year's Eve

Roses are red on Valentine's Day and so is
Champagne (made from costars Chardonnay and
Pinot Noir, with a supporting role played by Pinot
Meuniere). Many people celebrate with
Champagne or bubbly on Valentine's (and New
Year's), so these occasions are the perfect excuse
to kick it up a notch with rosé Champagne. You
may have thought it's out of your price range, but
it can be an affordable wine. It's almost a secret,
but rosé Champagne is a wonderful all-around
food wine too, especially delicious with other
"pink" foods like salmon and lamb. The beautiful
color and special flavor are due to the extra dose
of Pinot Noir in the blend. Read on to find a rosé
sparkler to fit your budget:

SPARKLING

Freixenet Brut Rosé (Spain, non-vintage $11)

Gratien & Meyer Cuvee Flamme Brut Rosé
(Loire Valley, non-vintage, $18)

Domaine Chandon Brut Rosé
(California, non-vintage, $20)

Roederer Estate Brut Rosé
(California, non-vintage, $25)

Iron Horse Brut Rosé
(California, non-vintage, $28)

S. Anderson Brut Rosé
(California, non-vintage, $36)

*Non-vintage, or NV, means the grapes that went
into making the wine aren't from one harvest year
but are a blend of several years. Sparklers can also
be made from higher quality grapes that come*

from one harvest that has the vintage year listed on the label.

CHAMPAGNES

Nicholas Feuillatte Premier Cru Brut Rosé (non-vintage, $35)

Pommery Brut Rosé (non-vintage, $45)

Billecart Salmon Brut Rosé (non-vintage, $60)

Jacquesson Signature Rosé (non-vintage, $80)

Veuve Clicquot La Grand Dame Brut Rosé (1995, $150)

Krug Rosé (non-vintage, $215)

Louis Roederer Cristal Brut Rosé (1995, $300)

Bollinger Vieilles Vignes Francaises (1988, $370)

Weddings and Anniversaries

These occasions always bring up the issue of whether or not to serve a sparkling wine or Champagne. (Only bubbly from the Champagne region in France may be called Champagne.) They are usually incorrectly served with a piece of sweet cake, and virtually no one in this kind of situation is paying attention to the wine. All that guests expect is that it should have bubbles. That's why I urge people to stick with sparkling wines at about $10 to $15 a bottle—Cava from Spain, Cremant de Loire from France, or a Californian or Australian sparkling wine.

How to Make a Toast

A section on special occasions and wine wouldn't be complete without mentioning the age-old ritual of toasting. I am on a mission to reform our toasting habits, which have become woefully sloppy. The truly proper form for a toast, which is the way the Europeans still do it and which we ragtag Americans have dispensed with, is as follows. After the preamble in which the toaster describes his relation to the honoree(s), the importance of the occasion, and something special about the honoree(s), the toaster recites the actual toast—a brief, easy to remember phrase, like, "To Margaret and Henry, may they have lifelong happiness"—and then invites the audience to raise their glasses and repeat the toast in unison back to the couple. In Europe, this is authentic toasting, and everyone is involved. On this side of the pond, we tend to extremes. We either just look at each other, say, "Cheers," and clink glasses, or an individual goes on and on, often telling bawdy jokes or devolving into long, tear-jerking anecdotes. So I

Why Toast?

The word "toasting" began with the custom of adding a piece of toasted bread (crouton) to a glass of wine to improve the flavor and to absorb the sediment that unavoidably floated in the glass.

Toasting first became fashionable in England in the early 1600s. In those days, the host would be the first to rise, saying, "Before we drink to the happy couple, let us make a toast." That was the cue to drop a crouton in your glass. To keep the revelers occupied while the bread was doing its job, the host would say a few words, trying to be witty, amusing, or at least sincere. The concluding "To Margaret and Charles!" was a signal to remove the crouton and repeat the toast, then drink. Not only phrases but short limericks and Shakespearean sonnets were the rage. And even after Madame Veuve Clicquot and her cellar master discovered how to get the sediment out of a bottle of Champagne in the 1830s, the phrase "to toast" lived on to this very day.

beg you to practice the proper form and spread good toasting across the country.

Wine Tastings: Do Try This at Home

Wine tastings, whether in public or private, should be fun. They are not lectures, nor are they a competitive arena for beating your companions in guessing which wine is which. Wine tastings *may* be educational as well as entertaining, but I believe in entertainment first, education second. Consider these variations on the wine tasting theme if you'd like to hold one at home.

1. **Open Tasting.** No secrets, no fooling. Just pour each sample and discuss. If you're in charge (and I certainly hope you'll feel confident stepping into this role after you've read my book), give people time to make up their own minds about the wine before you comment. Tasting again after comments will help everyone learn from each other's observations.

2. **Paired Tasting.** Taste a pair of wines and notice any contrast. This can be as diverse as Cabernet Sauvignon versus Pinot Noir, Pinot Noir from California versus Pinot Noir from France. If you want a more advanced tasting, try the same wine from different vintages or the same type but produced differently such as oaked versus unoaked Chardonnay. (See below for an in-depth description of a fascinating paired tasting.)

3. **Blind Tasting.** You can make this tasting as easy or hard as you want it to be. Blind tasting Chardonnay versus Sauvignon Blanc is relatively easy since the wines have such

different flavors and alcohol levels. Tasting the subtle differences between vintages of the same wine is hard since the differences are a result of the growing conditions in each of the vintage years. The point is to rely solely on the taste and smell experience without the influence of label by covering the bottle. Most professional tasting is done blind for this reason.

4. Price Comparison. One of the most fun tastings I do is to blind taste the same type of wine at different price points. When I tell participants that the three wines in front of them are essentially the same except for price (same type, same vintage), they really concentrate so as to be able to identify the better quality/higher cost wine. Discovering that you can't tell the difference or prefer the lesser priced wine may be a shock, but it'll be good for the pocketbook the next time you are buying wine.

These are only basic formats; they can be varied endlessly. If you dip into tastings, make sure that you and other participants agree on how serious you want to be. No matter what kind of tasting you hold, you should have two glasses for each person, a spit bucket or two, and water and plain crackers for palate cleansing. Don't taste more than six wines. More than that and the tasting turns into a drinking party—maybe fun for frat boys, but not what you intended. I think it's a lovely gesture to send your guests home with a list of the wines they tasted, including prices and where to buy them.

There are a few things it's good to know or practice before hosting your first wine tasting. We were taught how to hold a fork and knife growing up, but few of us have grown up in a household where our parents showed us how to hold a wineglass. Sorry to say, most people don't know that the correct way to hold a wineglass is by the stem for both aesthetic and practical reasons. Not only is it a matter of good form, but it prevents the glass from getting full of greasy fingerprints. The practical reason for not picking up the wine by the bowl is that the warmth from our hands warms up the wine.

Once you're holding the glass correctly, you might think you are ready to drink the wine. Not so fast. I recommend a three-step approach. First, swirl the wine in the glass. The aromas rise and are suspended at the top of the glass for just a few seconds. Step two, therefore, is to plunge your nose into the glass, inhaling as you do so. Someone once said, "Drinking wine is like cooking, you need to get your nose in the saucepan in order to know what's going on." Then, and only then, take a small sip . . . and savor.

Wine, Women, and Song

Wine has been used since at least ancient Egyptian times for both religious rituals and plain old partying. In a crude form, it goes all the way back to 8,500 BC, when Neolithic humans apparently drank a version made from fermented fruit. For much of history, however, it was the drink of the wealthy, ruling classes. Aboard ships of the British Royal Navy, for example, wine was served only to officers, and grog (a mixture of rum and water) was given to the crew. Among royalty and diplomats, arriving at important decisions—electing leaders, deciding matters of war or peace, and marriages—were always celebrated with wine. Isn't it wonderful that today even we simple folk can use wine whenever we want?

The Gift of Giving

One of the toughest wine-buying challenges is in giving gifts. When you want to bring a bottle of wine to a dinner party, for instance, knowing what to buy can be tricky. Do you know what the menu is? Will your hosts serve your wine or tuck it away for some other time? If you want to bring a wine and have it served at the dinner party, ask your hostess in advance. If she agrees, you will get your wish, but if not, you won't be disappointed at the party. Do you know the wine preferences of your hosts? Are the guests wine lovers who would appreciate an intriguing or unusual selection? The answers to all these questions will narrow down your choice. One general caution: If you bring a white, don't buy it already chilled. It might have been sitting in the store's cooler for months. Chill it before you arrive, and if you are in a hurry, just put it into an ice bucket with salty water and ice for ten minutes.

I recommend picking from one of the following four categories:

1. **Prom Queen.** Everyone loves Champagne. It comes in all price points and can be served as an aperitif, with the meal, or with fruit desserts (not cake or chocolate, please, unless you get the sweeter styles labeled *demi-sec* or *doux*).

2. **Blind Dates.** When you don't know what your hosts are serving yet you think they may want to pour your wine, bring wines that go with a wide range of foods. Some great choices in pairing wines are:

   • Sauvignon Blanc (New Zealand)

   • Sancerre (Sauvignon Blanc from France)

   • Pinot Gris (France, Oregon)

   • White Bordeaux (Sauvignon Blanc/Semillon blend from France)

- Pinot Noir (California, Oregon)

- Red Burgundy (Pinot Noir from France)

- Shiraz (Australia)

- Côtes du Rhône (France)

- Rioja (Spain)

- Chianti (Italy)

3. **Show-offs.** Distinctive whites like Albariño from Spain, a Grüner Veltliner from Austria, or a Vouvray from France will impress the recipients. Or bring a gorgeous redhead from Spain's Ribera del Duero region, a Taurasi from southern Italy, or a Pinotage from South Africa. Caution! Do this only if your hosts are open to trying new things.

4. **Sweet Innocents.** Dessert wines finesse the question of pairing your wine with the host's menu. Examples that are under $20 include Moscato d'Asti, Oloroso Sherry, Muscat de Beaumes-de-Venise, Montbazillac, and Cadillac, which are Sauternes-style wines, Madeira (Malmsey grapes), and Hardy's Whisker's Blake, a Port-like wine from Australia made from Shiraz grapes.

One absolute caveat: Do not bring an expensive bottle that is too young to be served at tonight's dinner party. Your host may be tempted to open it as a favor to you, but both of you will be guilty of "wine infanticide." It is not only a waste of a potentially great taste experience that will emerge only in later years, but chances are this young, immature wine won't taste very well tonight—a double disappointment. (See page 170–171 for wines that benefit from aging.) At the same time, do try to bring a wine that's a bit unusual. In other words, even if you get a Chardonnay, buy one that you don't see every day. If you are asked to bring wine for the whole gathering, the rule of thumb is that there are six glasses to a bottle. The Wine Diva says to estimate a half bottle per person. It's better to have too much than too little.

The Grace of Receiving

If you are in the delightful position of being on the receiving end, equal etiquette applies. If your guest has followed the preceding advice, you need simply say, "Thank you." But what if a guest just shows up bottle in hand without any advance warning? "Thank you" is still the appropriate response, but then you need to do more. First, look at the label. Is this a wine you could consider using at tonight's dinner? If you can gracefully substitute it for one you've already selected, ask the gift giver, "Would you like me to serve this tonight?" In the case of the wine not working— either with your menu or your standards—you might say, "That is so thoughtful of you. I've already set aside the wines for tonight, but I'm sure we'll find a time to enjoy this one soon." If the spirit moves you, you can extend an invitation to join you at a later date to drink the wine. No matter whether the wine is a super Tuscan or sheer plonk, remember it's the thought that counts.

The Wine Diva's Most Popular Tasting

And now I'm going to share with you the tasting that is most often requested by my corporate clients. It's based on styles of wine, not brands, so you can easily duplicate it at home. First you need a tiny bit of background.

By now you've learned that wine can be categorized in many ways—white or red, light or heavy, dry or sweet, oaked or unoaked, French or Italian. Another distinction I find extremely user friendly is New World versus Old World wines. As you may guess, the Old World encompasses European wines from France, Italy, Spain, and Germany, where the winemaking tradition has evolved over many, many centuries. New World wines are made in California, Chile, Argentina, Australia, New Zealand, and anywhere else where the wine business started to lift off in the past fifty years or so.

In this tasting you compare New World and Old World wines made from the same grape. The purpose of this novel side-by-side comparison is to help you discover and appreciate the differences. California epitomizes the New World style of winemaking: bold fruit flavors, strong oaky aromas, and high alcohol. Fans of this style love these fruit bombs. France stands for the Old World style: subtle, subdued fruit, restrained oak, moderate alcohol, and more complex flavors that are revealed as the wine evolves. You'll remember the difference easily if you picture a big, over the top, loud American talking to an elegant, understated, philosophical French woman. Another memory aid is that New World names for wines are the name of the grape. Old World wines are most often called by the name of the place where the grapes are grown.

Fans of the Old World style, like me, feel these wines have more character and are more food friendly. You may find you like both styles equally well. Fortunately, wine stores are like the U.N. and you can find wines of every nationality to suit every taste.

Oftentimes, people are surprised that they like the Old World style better than the New World style they are used to. Knowing this may be a trend, many California winemakers are making wines in the Old World style. They think that lower alcohol, more subtle wines are better food partners. At the same time, some Old World winemakers in France, Italy, and Spain are trying to broaden their appeal in the international wine market and so they make their wine in a New World—or "new wave"—style.

What this tasting will teach you is which style you prefer. Then when you shop at the store or speak with the sommelier, you can sound knowledgeable and authoritative, communicate precisely what you like, and get it! You can say, "Are any of the California Chardonnays on your wine list made in the Old World style? Do you carry any 'new wave' Riojas, Barolos, or Bordeaux in your store?"

So, now you know everything you need to have your New World versus Old World wine tasting party. Be sure to taste both styles of wine with and without food. Here are the wines that you could include:

WHITES

California Chardonnay and white Burgundy (France)

New Zealand Sauvignon Blanc and Sancerre or Pouilly Fumé (France)

Oregon Pinot Gris and Pinot Gris from the Alsace region in France

Australian or California Riesling and Riesling from Alsace or Germany

REDS

California Pinot Noir and red Burgundy
(France)

Australian Shiraz or California Syrah and
French Syrah

This is your chance to shine, so give your
guests the overview of the tasting's goal and what
they are trying to taste. Put all the wine in brown
bags with numbers in the front and make a chart
so you'll remember which is which: 1A *vs* 1B, 2A
vs 2B, etc. Print handouts with a description of
Old World and New World, a list of the
corresponding numbers, and a space to jot down
if they think a wine is Old World or New World.
Then they can also circle the wine they liked the
best. At the bottom of the page, note the names
and prices of all the wines so friends can look for
these same wines if they fall in love.

Be sure to have buckets, big plastic cups, or
some opaque container on the table near the
bagged bottles of wine so people can pour out the
wine they can't drink in order to taste the next
pair of wines.

Try not to have guests drink on an empty
stomach and have cheese and crackers or bread
available.

When you reveal the wines, you'll be
surprised at how many people can identify
correctly the Old World wine versus the New
World wine. After each pairing, ask the group
how many preferred the New World style and
how many preferred the Old World style. At the
end, ask how many people stayed with the
California New World style they know and love.
How many switched over and now prefer the Old
World style?

You could really intrigue your guests by telling them that many of the California, Oregon, and other New World producers are now making wine in the Old World style. Bring out a few of these wines—hidden, of course—in those handy brown bags. Explain they are the "extra credit" wines and let them taste. If anyone can tell the difference between California Chardonnay made in the Old World style or true Old World Chardonnay—from Burgundy in France—they are ready to graduate to the next class of wine tasting.

The Morning After

You've had a memorable holiday, wine tasting, or gourmet restaurant dinner, with wonderful red wine, and you go to bed glowing. But the next day, you wake up with a killer headache. You've heard it's something about the sulphites in red wine that cause headaches and vow to resist red wine from now on. It ain't necessarily so. For most people, the sulphites in red wines are *not* the culprit. White wines actually have more sulphur added to them than red wines.

Here's the scoop on how you can avoid so-called "red wine" headaches. Do NOT do any of the following:

1. **Drink wine if you are sensitive to histamines.** This is likely the biggest reason for your headaches. Histamines are a natural part of red wines, and taking an antihistamine pill several hours before you know you will be drinking red wine may well solve the problem. If you have any concerns about histamines in general, ask your doctor.

2. **Drink wine on an empty stomach.** The more food you eat, the less likely it is that you will get a headache.

3. **Drink wine when you are dehydrated.** Common sense: Drinking water dilutes whatever is causing you problems.

4. **Drink wine when you are especially fatigued.** If you tossed and turned the night before, this can affect whether you succumb to a headache.

One other cause of headaches is the tannins in red wines. Experimentation can help you determine which wines to avoid and what works best, so you don't feel compelled to give up drinking red wine completely. First, try red wines low in tannin, beginning with Beaujolais Nouveau and Beaujolais-Villages, with the lowest amount of tannin, and continuing in order of tannin with Barbera, Bardolino, Valpolicella, Dolcetto, Pinot Noir, Saumur Champigny, Chinon, Bourgueil, and Cabernet Franc. You'll learn which wines you tolerate and which trigger a headache.

Tannins in full-bodied red wines that have at least five to eight years bottle age have mellowed and may not be as likely to cause headaches. Finally, if all else fails, turn to unoaked white wines like Sauvignon Blanc, Pinot Grigio, Muscadet, Pinot Gris, Albariño, Sancerre, Pouilly-Fumé, and Pinot Blanc. These white wines contain no tannin because they aren't aged in oak barrels (which leach tannin into the wine); and white grapes don't contain tannin in their skins as red grapes do.

Storing
Your *Wine*

W ho would buy ice cream for dinner tomorrow with no freezer in which to store it overnight? So it should be with wine. Storing wine can mean anything from where to stash that bottle you just brought home from the supermarket to having your latest purchases hand-trucked to the proper section of your vast wine cellar. It all depends on how serious you are about wine and how much you have to store. But no matter how big or small the need, there are two C's that apply when considering how to store wine: conditions and convenience.

Conditions

If you are wondering what difference storage conditions make, consider the fact that damage to wine from improper storage is cumulative. That is, the longer the exposure to bad conditions, the more likely it is that the expensive old treasure you bought on your honeymoon in France will turn to vinegar. The signs that this may be happening range from bad to worse.

- Dry, flaking cork is NOT GOOD.

- Oozing red sticky stuff around the neck of the bottle is BAD.

- Evaporation inside the bottle resulting in a lower fill level (called ullage) is VERY BAD.

If you notice any of these signs, drink immediately. If you are lucky, the wine will still be alive enough to enjoy.

But there are simple ways you can prevent your wine from "going off," as wine experts sometimes say. I've already described how stores should keep bottles at their best while stored on the shelf: Lay them on their sides, provide reasonably constant, cool temperatures (ideally 60 to 65 degrees, attics and garages being strictly off limits), don't expose them to strong light. (Rather like how an aging diva wants to be treated.) The same principles hold true for storing wine at home, but with two added caveats.

First, be sure no vibrations from washing machines, refrigerators, nearby trains, or other sources can upset your delicate bottles. Second, do not store wine—especially Champagne—in the refrigerator. I know this may come as a surprise, but it turns out that refrigeration actually *dries out* its contents. Lettuce, for example, stays nice and crisp in the fridge because it is dry. If it were a moist environment, the lettuce would wilt. Well, that same dryness applies to wine corks. And once a cork is too dry, it's susceptible to shrinking and letting in the enemy, namely air. Heaven forbid! So do not store your wine in the fridge for more than two weeks, tops. If you have Champagne languishing in the back of the refrigerator while you wait for something to celebrate, wait no more. Drink it tonight and celebrate never letting a good bottle go bad again!

If you happen to live in a house with a basement, you have a built-in cellar. This area is underground—dark, with cool and more constant temperatures. If you don't have a basement, store your wine at the bottom of a closet or under a bed.

Naturally, the Wine Diva knows of a few more sophisticated wine storage conditions, but this is all you need to remember.

Convenience

The convenience factor for having wines safely stored in your home is the same as it is for your spices. Imagine if every time you cooked dinner, instead of having salt and pepper at the ready, or oregano on the top shelf, you had to run to the store and figure out what to buy (and hope they had what you want). You'd never want to cook! To enjoy wine with your meals at home, make it easy on yourself. If you don't invest in a wine cellar, I recommend that you keep a small supply—one dozen is a minimum—of wines for everyday use close at hand. Include a few bottles of better wines and bubbly in case company suddenly appears or a forgotten birthday or anniversary surfaces.

The Case for a Cellar

Doesn't the mere phrase *wine cellar* conjure a grand estate in the hedgerowed Hamptons of New York or the English countryside? But just what is a wine cellar anyway? If the idea sounds too swanky for you, let me clarify. By cellar I simply mean a dedicated place to keep your wines under good conditions for an extended period of time (a year or more). Sounds straightforward enough, right? Here's why I encourage you to explore the wonderful world of wine cellars:

The Good Stuff Is Always in Short Supply

Your best chance of actually obtaining a great bottle of wine is always when it first goes on sale. The problem is that these gems are not ready to drink at that young age. Buying early and storing for later drinking is not only a good investment, it assures you that when you want that special wine, it will be ready and waiting in your cellar.

Graceful Aging

While 90 percent of the wines produced in the world are meant to be consumed in the first year or two, about 9 percent can be cellared and offer you the same wonderful aromas and flavors after five to six years. These are the premium varietal wines we buy for approximately $25 to $40—Chardonnay, Pinot Noir, Merlot, Syrah, Zinfandel, and Cabernet.

A small number, just 1 percent of red and white wines, actually improve with age to gain extra layers of flavors that make them more complex. As the reds age, their deep color lightens, their fruitiness and oakiness fades, and their rough, tannic edges soften. While this happens, other flavors evolve that might be earthy, woodsy, or meaty. These reds take six to eight years to reach that "plateau of maturity" and then can last for a decade or more in the best vintages. Ageworthy reds include:

> AUSTRALIA: Top Cabernet Sauvignon and Shiraz

CALIFORNIA: Top Cabernet Sauvignon and Zinfandel

FRANCE: Bordeaux of Cru Bourgeois quality and upward, Burgundy of premier cru and grand cru quality levels, Rhônes such as Hermitage and Cote Rotie

ITALY: Barolo, Brunello di Montalcino, and Super Tuscans

SPAIN: Tempranillo-based wines from Ribera del Duero

There are also a few white wines that can become more complex with age In the best vintages, such as:

AUSTRALIA: Top Chardonnay, Riesling, and Hunter Valley Semillon

CALIFORNIA: Top Chardonnay

FRANCE: Bordeaux from Pessac-Leognan area, Burgundy of premier cru and grand cru quality levels, Riesling and late harvest wines from Alsace

Sweet dessert wines benefit from age as well: Port from Portugal, Sauternes from France, and Riesling BA and TBA from Germany (feel free to say BA and TBA to sub for their long and difficult to pronounce wine names).

If you're lucky enough to have bought a case of the same wine, you can reward your patience by opening a bottle every three to four years and discovering how it's changing and improving.

Return on Investment

Wine sellers know that wines from good vintages are worth more as they near their peak drinking years and prices rise accordingly. For example, Bordeaux Superieurs from the 2000 vintage first appeared on shelves at prices ranging from $10 to $13. The price for those same wines in 2005 was $14 to $19, a more than 40 percent increase. In that same time period, top-tier classified Bordeaux doubled or tripled in price. So consider buying and cellaring some of the finer reds. You can save yourself good money over time. The return on your investment probably won't compare to that of real estate, but who can drink a beach house?

Bargain Cellars, Not Bargain Basement

Certain stores deal in close-outs, purchased collections, and other one-time opportunities. One merchant I deal with offers 30 percent off for ten days once per year. By making space for storing wine you can take advantage of buying whenever an attractive opportunity, such as a special sale, arises. Wouldn't it be a shame not to have room for a delicious bargain?

Another kind of opportunity is stocking up on cases once you find a wine you want as part of your regular repertoire. Experiment, then find the best price on a wine that you like and put it away!

How Much Wine Should You Store?

I can only answer that question if I know your intentions, and I don't mean whether they're honorable or not. Is your motivation strictly utilitarian, in the same way you store extra food in the freezer? Or are you a proud collector whose primary interest is showing wines to admiring guests? I have met people who have let their cellars become an obsession. They buy wines, store them in remote places, and enjoy their treasures by poring over the inventory pages of their carefully annotated cellar books. Some collectors have reasons for buying huge quantities of wines that are more the province of psychologists than wine divas!

Those with a more practical bent can think about the following three points in deciding how much wine to store at any given time.

The Cost of Storage

A cellar that holds a thousand bottles costs more to build than one that holds only a hundred or so. But also think about the inventory cost. If Champagne taste and a beer budget applies to you, start with a home mini-cellar so that you always have a dozen bottles on hand. Once the noble grape takes hold, you'll start adding bottles, filling up the space under the bed, then closet floors, entire closets, and eventually a special wine fridge that holds about sixty bottles, which will never be enough, because by now . . . you're hooked! I even turned one of my two clothes closets into wine storage so I could have anything I wanted at hand and, I confess, just to gaze appreciatively at it. When I outgrew even the closet, I took space at a professional storage facility and got "visitation rights" to my wine. Collecting wine had become such an obsessive treasure hunt that my husband, Max, finally said, "Why wines and not shoes like every other woman?" When your husband compares you unfavorably with Carrie in *Sex and the City*, that's obsessive!

If you are just starting out, a budget of $300 a year for about twenty bottles will grow your cellar (assuming you also replace what you are drinking) at an affordable rate and over time will allow you to upgrade the quality as well. When you are not increasing the number of bottles in storage, your $300 budget allows you to upgrade as you replace.

The Options Factor

Doing your own tasting "homework" is an essential part of accumulating a wine cellar that *you* will enjoy. After all, this is your cellar and, like the art on your walls, it should reflect your taste. As the saying goes, "There's no substitute for pulling corks." Get some help from your friendly merchant or from a friend whose knowledge and taste may give you a short list to consider and then taste your way to your best, customized cellar.

Meanwhile, since most white wines are not suitable for long-term storage or benefit from it, let's focus on the reds you will be storing. Think about how you usually order when you are in a good restaurant. You likely are never going to have as much variety in your cellar as you would find on a quality wine list, nor do you need to.

The first goal is to have wines at the ready no matter what you are having for dinner. Refer to the food and wine pairings chapter for some help in this matter. Make your cellar choices—whether medium bodied Pinot Noirs or huskier, full-bodied Cabernets—match the food you most often like to serve and you can't go wrong as you build the foundation of your cellar.

After your foundation is sound, you can build a nice frame by expanding beyond Cabernets or Pinot Noirs. I believe any cellar worth its salt should include French and Italian wines. Your tasting excursions into other producing regions may inspire you to fill out your collection from Spain, Portugal, Australia, Argentina, or even more exotic regions. Ideally you will have at least two bottles of any one choice. This means you can select any wine from your cellar for a dinner group of four or more. It also allows you to try a wine a second time to decide if you want to replace it or not.

Your Rate of Consumption

How do you figure out how much wine to store in order not to deplete your cellar? Do a little math and calculate your annual usage in these five categories:

- Everyday

- Company

- Gifts

- Party

- Special occasion

Let's say a wine-loving couple, the Grapenuts, is ready to invest in a real cellar and want to decide how large it should be. They both work full-time and dine out several times a week. With a wide circle of friends, they entertain often at intimate dinner parties and a couple of large affairs a year. Their hospitality is reciprocated, so they have regular occasions to give wine as gifts.

Everyday

If the Grapenuts eat out and only have dinner at home three times a week, that means they should have one case of red and a case of white on hand for everyday drinking wine. They will need to restock every five to six weeks, so the everyday category starts with twenty-four bottles. At an average price of $12 per bottle, the Grapenuts' initial investment in this category is $288.

Company

The Grapenuts have friends over to dinner eight times a year and use four bottles per dinner, or thirty-two bottles. Average price for this bunch is a bit more, say $18 or an investment in dinner wines of $576.

Gift

The Grapenuts give ten bottles of wine as gifts throughout the year at an average price of $15, or $150 in total. Some people give more expensive wines, but I believe the more thoughtful gift is a wine the recipients love and discover is affordable enough to buy themselves for everyday use.

Party

The Grapenuts host an annual Christmas party for about sixty of their friends. At two to three glasses per guest, they buy about three cases for the party and spend $500.

Special Occasion

For their one special occasion a year, the Grapenuts need six bottles. They usually budget $150 or so for this festive anniversary. The Wine Diva says if it is really a special occasion such as an anniversary or your spouse's birthday, don't skimp. Serving a $10 mass-produced wine at your twenty-fifth anniversary party sends the wrong message about the state of your connubial bliss. If your anniversary is worth celebrating, do it in style.

So, the Grapenuts' ideal cellar would have eight cases, or a hundred bottles, and cost $1,600—not bad for the hours and hours of drinking pleasure those beautiful bottles will afford you.

The Affordable Wine Cellar

Does spending less but drinking better wine sound good to you? Here are seven strategies for collecting wines to store at reasonable prices.

1. Buy everyday table wines you can drink immediately.

Not all wines improve with age. Taste wines under $15 a bottle, whose youthful fruitiness will only decline with time. Don't cellar too many of them—keep restocking so they are fresh. Examples: Sauvignon Blanc, Pinot Grigio, Pinot Blanc, and Beaujolais-Villages.

2. Buy "weekend" wines for company now and in the future.

Wines costing $25 to $40 a bottle can be enjoyed now but will benefit from time in the bottle. Premium-priced Cabernet, Pinot Noir, and Syrah fit this category, as well as Bordeaux's cru Bourgeois. My favorite cru Bourgeois are Château Pontensac and Château d'Aiguilhe.

3. Buy special occasion wines for a later date.

Buying Barolo, Brunello, and classed growth Bordeaux doesn't have to mean remortgaging the house. Simply put: Buy now, drink later. Buy them as soon as they are available for about $50 to $75 a bottle. They won't be drinkable then, but hold them five years or more. Then start enjoying them as they increase in complexity and value.

4. Buy the "wanna-be" wines.

Seek out wines from up-and-coming areas adjacent to famous vineyards. These well-made wines are easy on the wallet and offer real value. The St-Émilion "satellites" and Lalande de Pomerol are good examples of vineyard areas producing quality Merlot-based wines with all the style of their tonier neighbors from St-Émilion and Pomerol, but without the high prices.

5. Buy famous wines in poor vintages.

World-class wine producers have to ruthlessly cull out poor grapes in off vintages to make good wines. Their loss is your gain. In 1991, 1992, and 1993 only a few producers on the left bank of Bordeaux (Cabernet-based wines) made superior wine. In these same years, as well as in 1996 and 2002, this happened on Bordeaux's right bank (Merlot-based wines). You can find these vintages of top red Bordeaux at auction and online, at very reasonable prices. Even these less than perfect wines are still greater than most others on earth.

6. Buy second labels of famous wines in good vintages.

Buy the lesser labels of the premium wines that have some of the style of the "grand vin" but don't carry the high price tags of their prestigious relatives. Upon release, Carruades de Lafite sells for about one third the price of its more famous brother Chateau Lafite.

7. Buy wines from less familiar wine regions.

Try, for example, Malbec from Argentina; Spain's answer to Cabernet: Tempranillo-based wines like Pesquera; and South Africa's Pinotage.

Racks and Bins

To store wine bottles properly on their sides and keep their corks moist, you could resort to tipping the shipping cases on their sides. But a random pile of cardboard boxes isn't very pleasing to the eye, nor is it very secure. A better way to keep bottles in the preferred position is some kind of rack or bin system. If you do have a built-in cellar it should always contain bins and/or racks. Bins are big squares that contain an entire case of wine. Sometimes they are divided into triangles if you have less than twelve bottles of a particular wine. Racks allow each bottle to rest in a separate compartment on its side. If you don't have a custom cellar you do need to buy racks and/or bins, which store wines on their sides. Otherwise when you pull a bottle out from the middle or the bottom you'll have a domino effect of shifting bottles on your hands. It will disturb their sleep! If the wines are going to be stored under the bed, you can probably only accommodate two or three layers anyway, so forget racks or bins. There are plenty of these racks/bins in catalogues or housewares stores. I am partial to the add-on racking systems that allow for expanding your collection without rebuilding the racks from scratch.

Keeping Track of Your Wine

It's important to know your inventory. You don't want a bottle whose life span has peaked to lie unnoticed and unconsumed. Otherwise, you might have to "drink it up or give it a funeral!" as one wit once said. I began by using old-fashioned index cards at the top of each bin to record the name of the wine. I'd cross out and update the quantity by hand each time I took out a bottle. When I became more computer literate, I switched to using Robert Parker's software program. It not only inventories my stash, but indicates when my particular styles of wines are within their optimum drinking window—for example "Drink 2008–2015."

Insuring Your Collection

Once you start amassing a significant amount of wine, you should check if your homeowner's policy covers loss from fire, flood, or earthquake. My policy didn't, so I bought a rider for an additional premium. Now I rest easy, knowing I'll be reimbursed at current market value, not the price I originally paid, if a loss occurs.

Cellar Accessories

These days, catalogues are jammed with a myriad of temperature and humidity controlled refrigerated "caves" and the gadgets to go in them, including table-mounted cork pullers, humidity gauges, leather-bound cellar logs, computer inventory control programs, alarms, and on and on. If you are becoming a true wine hobbyist, you may want to indulge. Just be aware that whatever enjoyment or convenience they bring, no gadget ever improved the taste of wine. My stellar cellar advice? Keep your wines cool and on their sides, keep replacing what you drink, keep it simple, and simply enjoy!

Wine-inspired Travel

Wines, like eggs, taste better in the country. Any wine lover who has traveled to any wine region, whether it's California, Bordeaux, or Tuscany, has a story about that wonderful bottle of wine they enjoyed with their true companion at sunset overlooking . . . you get the idea. There is no doubt that ambience counts. In this chapter I intend to tempt you to visit one or more of the wine-producing parts of the world for an unforgettable getaway.

When considering wine-related travel, the first question to ask yourself is whether visiting a wine region is your primary goal or a side trip on a sightseeing vacation or business junket. If wine is your travel focus, make sure your companions agree. Not everyone's idea of fun is trekking from one winery to the next to taste yet another group of Cabernets or comparing this Pinot Noir to that one. If visiting wineries is going to be a side trip, then planning other events or destinations— museums, cathedrals, restaurants, concerts, and the like—will make your winery visits more special

I remember a time I didn't take my own advice with disappointing results. One recent summer, my husband and I rented a farmhouse in

Tuscany with another couple we have traveled with many times before to European capitals. Our farmhouse was located just twenty-five minutes from Montalcino, with its fabulous wineries that produce the crown prince of Italian red wines, Brunello di Montalcino. I assumed when we visited Montalcino for lunch, everyone would want to take advantage of being able to taste these magnificent big red wines, participate in a progressive wine tasting at a *cave,* and even visit a wine estate. Wrong! I was so dejected when they decided they preferred to visit yet another hill town. No matter where we went sightseeing, the only wine-related activity was ordering wine with lunch and dinner. Not a problem when vacationing in Paris, London, or Rome, but a bummer in wine country. So talk to your group first to clarify and/or lobby for a wine stop!

Wine-related travel can be especially enjoyable when you build your trip around a celebration (anniversary or birthday, for instance) or sampling some of the local cuisine in one or more of the better restaurants. Food in wine country is generally wonderful, providing peak pleasure for your palate. Or you can time your trip to coincide with special events such as the marathon in Bordeaux or the running of the bulls in Pamplona (not recommended immediately after hitting a couple of wineries).

Good starting points for planning a wine trip are *Wine Spectator* and *Decanter*. These magazines regularly publish three-to-four-page wine destination guides that include wineries, hotels, restaurants, shopping, and local sightseeing. Compare this with typing in "wine travel" on a search engine and getting over thirty thousand entries on wine travel—too much information!

If you want to plan your own trip I recommend making a schedule and reservations at the wineries you wish to visit. In Napa Valley you don't need reservations at the biggest wineries. In my opinion visits to smaller, less well known wineries are more interesting, and you do need to reserve in advance. By calling ahead you may have an opportunity to chat with the owner and/or the winemaker. You may even be offered one or two wines not on the regular list, as well as a tour through the facilities. If you receive this treatment, be sure to thank your host and be aware that not everyone is so honored. And finally, I also recommend that you either have a designated driver for the tour or hire a car service. Drinking and driving is a no-no in wine country—and everywhere else, for that matter.

Preparation

Doing your homework before your trip is always a good idea. If you're planning to visit a winery where you will meet the winemaker or owner, know their names ahead of time, as well as a little about the winery itself. This small bit of research will do wonders in helping you engage them to discuss their wines and perhaps taste some of their most prized labels during your visit.

Agriculture and viticulture are kissing cousins, so dress is casual at every winery. Most cellars are a cool 60 to 65 degrees Fahrenheit, even on the hottest days, so a sleeveless top would definitely need a sweater or sweatshirt. Cellars are sometimes wet from the constant washing that goes on. Boots aren't needed, but leave your high-heeled Manolos in the car in favor of boat shoes or other comfortable walking shoes that don't mind the damp. I like to wear my sunglasses around my neck on a lanyard so that as I move from bright sun to darkened cellar I don't lose them. And lighten up your handbag—a stroll through the vineyards, a sherry bodega, or a Champagne cave can be a long walk.

Take Your Time

While it may seem like a good idea to cram in as many winery stops as possible each day, resist. Don't wear out your companions and yourself by overscheduling, or you risk turning wine tasting into distaste. You also have to allow for travel time from one stop to the next. Three wineries in one day are ideal but in no case more than four. Schedule fewer if you have the chance to chat with the winemaker or go into the vineyards. Tasting rooms generally are open from late morning until late afternoon. One stop before lunch and two afterward is plenty. If you are making appointments, allow enough time so that you don't have to rush and excuse yourself to leave for the next winery as if the next stop is more important. We've all had guests leave our parties early with that excuse, and vintners don't appreciate it any more than you do.

In the Tasting Room

Some tasting rooms in the larger wineries are pretty commercial. They charge for the tasting and have staffs that are about as well trained as waiters. Others are more family-like, the winery literally an extension of the owner's home. Your host may be the owner, winemaker, or a staff member who is knowledgeable and passionate about wine. In any case be respectful of your host and others in the tasting room. Good manners go a long way in your being treated well, and paying attention to what is being said about the wine is part of those good manners. Small children and cell phones are best left in the car or outside with an adult in charge. Remember the uncouth character in the 2005 film *Sideways* and his revolting behavior in the tasting room? That's the opposite extreme of how to behave.

Tasting Etiquette

When you begin your tasting, you will most likely be offered wines in a sequence—usually starting with light white wines and ending with the biggest reds. It's okay to skip one or more of these wines if you know that a particular wine style is not to your liking, but it's not okay to taste ahead while the staff person is explaining the wine that you omitted. Be patient and reconsider your opportunity to try something new. A small sip of a wine that you're convinced you won't like may surprise you. After all, this is what you came for, isn't it? To taste something new? So try it. You might like it. Ask about what you have tasted and learn what descriptions apply to what your tongue experienced. "I thought this last sample was dryer than the last. Why is that?" This question, or a similar one, will generate a discussion about the characteristics of the wine and an opportunity to retaste after the host's comments. Repeating this taste/discuss/retaste sequence will train you to understand these subtleties and turn you into a more informed buyer. A curious taster is welcome; uninformed criticism is not.

Tasting versus Drinking

Visiting three or four wineries in a day can involve a lot of samples—as many as five tastes per winery, or twenty in all. Aside from the risk of drinking and driving, which should be avoided altogether, your ability to taste and evaluate wines diminishes if you have drained every sample put in front of you. The answer is to swirl, smell, taste, and spit, not swallow. Swallowing in fact doesn't add anything to tasting. By the time wine has passed over your tongue it's given you all the taste information there is to be had. If you only smelled and never tasted at all you would have enjoyed most of the experience—that's how much your nose contributes to what's called "taste." That's because your palate can only detect bitterness, saltiness, sourness, and sweetness.

We have all been taught that spitting is crude, rude, and altogether unacceptable. Spitting wine samples at wineries is an exception. Every tasting room has one or more buckets for spitting the wine you just tasted. Use the bucket. If you don't spit, by the end of the day you won't be able to taste anything. In some European cellars spitting is permitted on the floor, and the leftovers are washed up as part of winery maintenance. Look to your host to see what is customary. I recommend periodically rinsing your mouth with water just to refresh. Crackers also help. They absorb the flavors from the previous taste and get your tongue ready for the next one. Don't worry about reusing the tasting glass. Once you have dumped the

Rudy blew a geiser when Johan winked at an ostrich who got his wicker hat out of hock.

Important villages in Germany's Rheinhessen region that produces top quality Riesling: Rudesheim, Geisenheim, Johannisberg, Winkel, Oestrich, Wicker, Hattenheim, Hochheim.

remains of the previous sample into the dump bucket, the amount of wine remaining in your tasting glass is inconsequential, and won't affect your ability to assess the next sample.

Guided Tours

There are tour operators in almost every wine-producing area and—like all tours—they are the easiest way to cover a lot of ground in a short time. Operators typically organize the itinerary, make the necessary appointments, provide the transportation and arrange food and lodging. Costs and quality vary significantly just as cruise lines do, so a little research ahead of time is required.

If you are of a mind to visit wine country either in the States or abroad, you have a lot of choices as to how to do it.

The first decision to make is whether or not to go with a tour group—either tagging onto an existing tour or hiring a guide for your group only. The first option is less expensive, but less flexible. Sometimes the tour is offered by a club, an alumni association, or other organization, in which case you have some idea of your fellow travelers. These trips have knowledgeable guides to discuss what you are going to see and taste as you travel. If you can find a tour that is the right length and goes where you think you would like to go, it's a good option.

In the second option, you can hire a tour guide for a whole trip or for one or two days only. My suggestion for finding a guide is good old word of mouth. Otherwise, start with a search engine. At last count there were almost four million choices under the heading *wine tour guides*. A personal guide costs more, but your tour will be fitted to your tastes and pace. A good guide may get you into wineries that are a little off the beaten path, as well as to lodging and dining that are not in every guide book. The key, of course, is the quality of the guide. Be sure to get references and talk to your potential guide to see if you're simpatico, especially as to your level of interest about the subject. Have in mind what your expectations are, what you want to learn, and at what pace. If you think your group can only visit two wineries in a day, tell the guide. If there are people in your group who can't do a lot of stairs, make sure that no descent into the *chais* two stories below the winery is on the "must see" list.

Here is a sampling of some of the more exotic tours and guides from the thousands available. See pages 203–204 for contact information on the following companies.

Arblaster & Clark Wine Tours Worldwide

This is the big name in escorted wine and gourmet tours. They offer a fascinating range of holidays that include a Champagne weekend, wine tours of Chile, South Africa, and New Zealand, walking tours of many classic wine regions, and a luxury wine cruise from Sicily to Greece.

Fine Wine Travel

As you cruise the high seas on luxury ships like Crystal Cruises, *Windstar,* Radisson *Seven Seas,* and the *Silversea* you can indulge your passion for fine wine, gourmet food, and interesting travel destinations while meeting like-minded travelers and learning from the world's leading experts.

Tasting Places

Forget the romantic weekend in Paris. Take me away on a white truffle and wine weekend in the Piedmont region in Italy! While Tasting Places normally runs hands-on cooking classes in stunning locations, including Thailand, they also offer this special no-cooking, gastronomic extravaganza.

Chateau Meyre, Bordeaux

For those who prefer to travel independently and stay in a luxurious château in the tranquil countryside—this is the experience for you! Plus they make reservations for tastings at prestigious wine estates so that you are warmly received as a welcomed guest rather than as a chance tourist.

Avalon Tours

This company can set up tours in any wine region in the world. They offer tours on preset dates that anyone can sign up for, or a package based on your travel dates can be customized.

Shop, Wine, and Dine

Join founder Anna Maria Sorrentino on trips to Italy's most exciting wine regions: Tuscany/Maremma, Piedmont, Campania, and Puglia. To ensure a high level of personal attention to each guest's needs, her tours are limited to a maximum of twelve people (minimum of four).

Gourmet Touring

Feeling debonair? Then tour Bordeaux in a 1970s Mercedes roadster. Whether just the two of you are celebrating a special occasion or your company wants to reward up to ten executives for excellent performance, Gourmet Touring offers a unique way to tour the vineyards via classic convertible sports cars such as the Mercedes Pagoda, the Barchetta, and Jaguar E-type.

Cellar Tours

Tailored tours for individuals, honeymooners, private groups, and companies. Private bilingual guides are *de rigueur*. Their clout extends to being able to arrange wine tastings of old and rare vintages of your preferred wines.

Fynbos Trails

Saddle up in South Africa for a half day (or more) on horseback, which allows you to experience the splendor of the Western Cape. If someone in the group is not inclined to horseback riding, they offer a range of private tours and specialized outings including garden tours, walking and hiking tours, as well as wine, olive, olive oil, and cheese tastings, and scenic drives.

Winery Driving Directions

Winery Bound (www.winerybound.com) is an online directory that offers driving directions and contact information for more than four thousand American wineries. The site lists wines for sale and winery events as well. You can look up wineries via maps, wine growing area name, or keyword. It's an excellent resource for reaching wineries for touring or direct sales.

Sleeping with the Vines

Most of the world's wine regions have beautiful hotels, inns, and B&Bs, but some people want to get closer to the action. Not content to gaze out on the vineyard ten feet away, they want to work in the winery—like being an extra in a movie in order to be on the set and mingle with the cast.

Wineries have always attracted wine lovers for tours and tastings, but until recently, few provided lodging within the actual winery. But now you don't have to settle for a glass of wine and a tour of the vineyard when you can stay at an inn on the winery grounds, which has the advantage that you don't need to taste and drive. Some, like the Rust Ridge Ranch Winery in Napa, will even let you lend a hand when the winery harvests its grapes in early fall.

Another cozy Napa B&B is Prager Winery & Port Works, a boutique winery set on thirty acres. They make varietal wines but specialize in port style fortified dessert wines.

For more listings of B&Bs in the United States, as well as unique lodgings abroad, such as Frank Gehry's new winery/hotel/spa at the Marques de Riscal winery in Rioja, please go to the Resources section on pages 203–204.

Wine Festivals

Wine festivals come in all shapes and sizes. One thing you can count on, though, is that you won't have to travel far to find one. At one time these festivals were held only in the wine country around harvest time—sort of a farmer's market; but they have now become year-round and are big deals. They are not only in big cities like New York, Dallas, Atlanta, Miami, and Chicago, but in small towns across America, as well as newer wine growing areas in southwest Michigan, northeast Ohio, "Heart of the Hill Country" in Texas, and the Shenandoah Valley in Virginia, to name just a few.

Wine festivals are organized by promoters who bring together the necessary ingredients including the venue for the event, the wineries and/or their distributors who will present wines for tasting, chefs and wine educators to give classes or seminars. Vendors of every kind of wine related merchandise, from corkscrews to magazines, sell their wares.

Venues vary from the beach, the ski slope, poolside, in the mountains, or among an entire village of old Victorian homes to cavernous wine caves, hotel ballrooms, and convention centers.

The atmosphere can vary from feeling like you are at a neighborhood church fair or homey summer camp to being inside the homes of the rich and famous. You'll definitely know when you read the material on each Web site whether it's appropriate to wear shorts and sneakers or if the crowd will be casually elegant.

Festivals may be one-day events or a three- or four-day weekend package. Larger festivals attract as many as two hundred wine vendors serving up to 1,700 wines (which seems like a never-ending parade!) with 25,000 people attending to those where attendance is limited to four hundred people to maintain a low-key, intimate atmosphere. The International Pinot Noir Festival is so popular that you have to sign up for its lottery, and only if your name is drawn are you extended an invitation to attend the festival, held on a college campus.

Attendance fees vary from $10 for small, single-day affairs to $300 for multiday events to $7,500 per couple to attend the Naples Winter Wine Festival and the Napa Valley Wine Auction over a long weekend. As the fees go up it's likely that a portion of the proceeds go to benefit a local charity. At smaller events costing $10 to $25 you'll walk around and taste at the different booths and cheese and crackers make do. As you spend more, say $30 to $300, the festival can include sit-down, tutored tastings, chef demonstrations, wine seminars, tasting portions of foods prepared by local restaurants, contests, and live entertainment. Contests can include anything from antique tractor races to wine spitting to wine bottle ring toss to grape stomping. Live entertainment ranges from rock 'n' roll, blues, country, and jazz to reggae, salsa, Cajun/Zydeco to hula music.

A worthwhile feature at many festivals these days is the reduced-price "designated driver" ticket. That person gets to enjoy the food and any of the seminars, but not imbibe. Be sure to find out if this is an option at the event you attend so you can plan in advance.

Some festivals are billed as "wine trails." They are self-guided tours going from one winery to the next in a fairly contained geographical area. Your ticket includes entry to all, but it's up to you how many you visit. Some organizers even chart scenic bike rides from one vineyard to the next.

Then there are the ritzy wine auction weekends in Naples, Florida, and in the Napa Valley that include lunches and dinners that will have you oohing and aahing. Celebrity vintners team up with some of the world's top chefs at intimate affairs held simultaneously at dozens of lavish private homes. Top vintners pour their coveted cuvées, which gives guests the opportunity to try highly rated cult wines that are normally available only to the fortunate few on the closed-out mailing lists or to big spenders at wine auctions and restaurants. While the Naples event is sold as a weekend package, you can purchase day tickets at the Napa event and enjoy a taste of this kind of festival.

The Grapes of Wreath

While many festivals give away the usual T-shirt or wineglass in the package price, the most unusual and special gift I've seen was a handmade grapevine wreath given to everyone who went on the "Heart of the Hill Country" wine trail in Texas. I collected a Christmas ornament at each of the sixteen wineries, and by the time I finished the trail my wreath was fully decorated. And what a good time I had doing it!

If you have never attended a festival, go to the Web site for the festival in question (almost all have Web sites) and read about what wines are being presented, what other activities are included, times, and costs. (See pages 195–198 for the names of the major festivals around the country.) Try one of the smaller events for your first time. They are more manageable and less expensive. If you enjoy the experience you can move on to the big time later, sort of like trying community theater before you spend $100 a ticket for a Broadway show.

Usually you can purchase wines at a festival, but that varies according to state law. Check first if you have your heart set on coming away with that unobtainable gem. There are usually no bargains to be had. My final advice is: Go early and if possible not on a weekend. Festivals can be fun but they can also be like trying to get a beer at the ball park—crowded stands, noisy, and wines in plastic cups. I like festivals because there are always new wines to taste and I love to hear all the latest wine world buzz.

Wine Festival Calendar

JANUARY

Boston, MA	Wine Expo
Mendocino, CA	Crab and Wine Days
Mohegan Sun, CT	The Sun Wine Fest
Russian River, CA	Wine Road, Winter Wineland Weekend
San Francisco, CA	Zinfandel Festival
Taos Ski Valley, NM	Winter Wine Festival

FEBRUARY

Buchanan, MI	Cupid's Arrow on the Southwest Michigan Wine Trail
Carmel, CA	Master of Food and Wine "Gourmet Olympics"
Hermann, MO	Chocolate Wine Trail in Missouri wine country
Miami, FL	South Beach Food and Wine Festival
Minneapolis, MN	Twin Cities Food and Wine Experience
Naples, FL	Winter Wine Festival
Newport, OR	Seafood and Wine Festival
Portland, OR	Seafood and Wine Festival
Yakima Valley, WA	Red Wine and Chocolate

MARCH

Cincinnati, OH	International Wine Festival
Columbia Valley, WA	Sweet Retreat
Monterey, CA	Wine Festival
Paso Robles, CA	Zinfandel Festival
San Francisco, CA	Rhône Rangers Wine Festival
Shell Beach, CA	World of Pinot Noir

APRIL

Austin, TX	Texas Hill Country Wine and Food Festival
Cary, NC	The Great Grapes Wine, Arts and Food Festival
Charlotte, NC	Food and Wine Weekend
Coral Gables, FL	International Wine Festival
Dallas, TX	Wine and Food Festival
Houston, TX	The Grand Wine and Food Affair

Key West, FL	Taste of Key West
Nashville, TN	L'Été du Vin Friends Auction
Las Vegas, NV	UNL Vino Wine Tasting
Los Olivos, CA	Santa Barbara Country Vintner's Festival
Sandestin, FL	Wine Festival
Sarasota, FL	Winefest and Auction
Seattle, WA	Taste of Washington
Vail, CO	Taste of Vail

MAY

Ann Arbor, MI	Wine Fest
Lebanon, TN	Toast to Tennessee
New Orleans, LA	Wine and Food Experience
Nantucket, MA	Wine Festival
Paso Robles, CA	Hospice du Rhône Wine Tasting
Paso Robles, CA	Wine Festival
Pittsburgh, PA	Wine Festival
Princeton, NJ	Great Grapes Wine, Arts and Food Festival
Shreveport, LA	Collector's Choice Wine Tasting and Auction
Washington, DC	Heart's Delight Wine Tasting and Auction

JUNE

Aspen, CO	Food and Wine Magazine Classic
Clayton, NY	New York State Food and Wine Festival
Cockeysville, MD	Great Grapes Wine, Arts and Food Festival
Detroit, MI	Food and Wine Festival
Fayetteville, AK	Art of Wine Festival
Lake Harmony, PA	Great Tastes of Pennsylvania
Napa Valley, CA	Wine Auction
San Francisco, CA	Pinot Noir Festival
Telluride, CO	Wine Festival
Washington, DC	International Wine and Food Festival

JULY

Altus, AK	Grape Fest
Amador County, CA	County FairWine Fair
Annapolis, MD	Great Grapes Wine, Arts and Food Festival
Hermann, MO	Cajun Concert on the Hill
Killlington, VT	Mountain Wine Festival
Maui, HI	Kapalua Wine and Food Festival
McMinnville, OR	International Pinot Noir Celebration
Santa Barbara, CA	Touring & Tasting Wine Magazine's California Wine Festival
Sonoma County, CA	Showcase of Wine and Food
Tanglewood, MA	Wine and Food Classic
Watkins Glen, NY	Finger Lakes Wine Festival

AUGUST

Long Island, NY	Wine Country
Key West, FL	Wine and Food Festival
Telluride, CO	Culinary Arts Festival

SEPTEMBER

Atlanta, GA	Wine South
Bernalillo, NM	New Mexico Wine Festival
Cape May, NJ	Food and Wine Festival
Chicago, IL	Windy City Wine Festival
Grapevine, TX	Grape Fest
Los Angeles, CA	American Wine and Food Festival
Naperville, IL	Wine Festival
Portland, CT	Taste of the World Wine and Food Festival
Red Hook, NY	Hudson Valley Wine Fest
Santa Fe, NM	Wine and Chile Fiesta
Saratoga, NY	Wine and Food Festival
Tri-Cities, WA	Harvest Festival and "Catch the Crush"
Tulsa, OK	Evening of Wine and Roses
Westminster, MD	Wine Festival

Wine Festival Calendar

OCTOBER

Caldwell, ID	A Taste of the Harvest
Charlotte, NC	Great Grapes Wines, Arts and Food Festival
Chicago, IL	Food and Wine Festival
Fredericksburg, TX	Food and Wine Fest
Hannibal, MO	Wine and Blues Fest
Lake Tahoe, NV	Autumn Food and Wine Festival
Longboat Key, FL	Stone Crab, Seafood, and Wine Festival
Miami, FL	Wine Fair
New Market, MD	Vintage Jazz Wine Festival
Norfolk, VA	Wine Festival
St. Louis, MO	Wine Festival
Scottsdale, AZ	First Press Fine Wine Auction
Sonoma, CA	Sonoma County Harvest Fair
Orlando, Fl	Epcot International Food and Wine Festival

NOVEMBER

Denver, CO	International Wine Festival
Joplin, MO	Wine Fest
Kohala Coast, HI	The Big Island Festival
Lake Michigan Shore, MN	Southwest Michigan Wine Trail
Las Vegas, NV	Las Vegas Odyssey
Monterrey, CA	Great Wine Escape Weekend and Auction
North Bend, OR	Oregon Coast Gourmet Fest
San Antonio, TX	New World Wine and Food Festival
San Diego, CA	Food and Wine Festival
Shenandoah Valley, VA	Deck the Halls Weekend
Sonoma County, CA	Russian River Wine Trail
Spokane, WA	Cork and Keg Festival
Temelcula, CA	Harvest WineTrail
Wilmington, DE	"Une Celebration du Vin" Auction
Yakima Valley, WA	Thanksgiving in Wine Country

DECEMBER

Anchorage, AK	Harvest of Wines
Fredericksburg, TX	Holiday Wine Trail
Austinburg, OH	Tannenbaum Wine Trail in Northeast Ohio
Yosemite National Park, CA	Vintners' Holidays

Although this book contains lots of useful lists and charts, they're not really what the Wine Diva is all about. Instead, I hope my practical tips, secrets, and shortcuts make you feel not only more comfortable with the subject of wine but downright enthusiastic about enjoying it regularly with meals. After all, as someone once said, and the Wine Diva wholeheartedly agrees, "A meal without wine is called breakfast." So from now on the key words connected to wine should be pleasure, enjoyment, and fun.

If after reading my book you are still drinking the same old wines rather than being adventurous and experimenting, I have failed you. If you are fearful rather than confident when you confront a wine list, I have more work to do. And if you are eager for more of the Wine Diva's opinions and advice, I promise a new book soon. . . .

Wine Diva Recommended Resources

Wine Books

Fear of Wine: An Introductory Guide to the Grape
by Leslie Brenner and Lettie Teague

Kevin Zraly's American Wine Guide by Kevin Zraly

Pairing Wine and Food: A Handbook for All Cuisines by
Linda Johnson-Bell

Sniffing the Cork: And Other Wine Myths Demystified by
Judy Beardsall with C. B. de Swaan

The Wine Avenger by Willie Gluckstern

*The Wine Lover's Cookbook: Great Recipes for the Perfect
Glass of Wine* by Sid Goldstein

Windows on the World Complete Wine Course
by Kevin Zraly

Wine for Dummies by Mary Ewing Mulligan, MW, and
Ed McCarthy

Wine Spectator's Essentials of Wine: A Guide to the Basics
by Harvey Steiman

Wine Travel Guide Books

*Discovering Wine Country: South of France, How to Find
Great Wines Off the Beaten Track* by J. Healey

*Discovering Wine Country: Bordeaux, How to Find Great
Wines Off the Beaten Track* by Monty Waldin

*Discovering Wine Country: Burgundy, How to Find Great
Wines Off the Beaten Track* by Patrick Matthews

*Discovering Wine Country: Northern Spain, How to Find
Great Wines Off the Beaten Track* by Susie Barrie

*Discovering Wine Country: Tuscany, How to Find Great
Wines Off the Beaten Track* by Monty Waldin

Northwest Wine Country: Wine's New Frontier
by Kathleen and Gerald Hill

Santa Barbara and the Central Coast: California's Riviera
by Kathleen and Gerald Hill

The Food and Wine Lover's Companion to Tuscany
by Carla Capalbo

The Best of Wine Country: A Witty, Opinionated and Remarkably Useful Guide to California's Vineyards by Don and Betty Martin

Wine Magazines

Wine Enthusiast www.wineenthusiast.com

Decanter www.decanter.com

Wine Spectator www.winespectator.com

Wine Accessories

Blue Hampton Picnic www.bluehamptonpicnic.com (205) 602-0257

International Wine Accessories www.iwawine.com (800) 527-4072

True Fabric www.truefabric.com (800) 750-8783

Wine Enthusiast www.wineenthusiast.com (800) 356-8466

Wine Label www.winelabel.com (800) 411-3732

Wine Merchandise www.winemerchandise.com (inquiries via their Web site only)

Wine Stuff www.winestuff.com (800) 946-3788

Wine Auctions

Acker Merrall & Condit www.ackerstore.com (877) 225-3747

Bonhams & Butterfield www.butterfields.com (415) 503-3363

Christie's www.christies.com (212) 636-2270

Morrell & Company www.morellwineauctions.com (212) 307-4200

Sotheby's www.sothebys.com (212) 606 7050

The Chicago Wine Company www.tcwc.com (847) 647-8789

Wine Bid www.winebid.com (888) 638-8968

Wine Commune www.winecommune.com
Inquiries via their Web site only

Zachys www.zachys.com (866) 922-4971

Wine Buying Online

Aabalat www.aabalat.com (707) 781-0619

Garagiste www.garagistewine.com (888) 264-0053

Garnet Wine www.garnetwine.com
(212) 772-3211

Morrell & Company www.morrellwine.com
(212) 688-9370

Premier Cru www.premiercru.net
(510) 655-6691

Sam's Wines & Spirits www.samswines.com
(800) 777-9137

Sherry-Lehmann www.sherry-lehmann.com
(212) 838-7599

Wine Library www.winelibrary.com
(888) 980-9463

Zachys www.zachys.com (866) 922-4971

Wine Cellars, Racks, Bins, and Refrigerated "Caves"

Vineyard Wine Cellars,
www.vineyardwinecellars.com (866) 973-1100

Wine Cellar Innovations
www.winecellarinnovations.com (800) 229-9813

Wine Racks of America
www.wineracksamerica.com (800) 373-6057

Wine Rack Superstore
www.wineracksuperstore.com (800) 987-5611

Wine Clubs

www.hartwickandgrove.com (866) 455-7207

www.winetasting.com (888) 540-9463

Wine Festivals

www.foodresource.com

www.gayot.com/events/main.html

www.localwineevents.com

www.starchefs.com

www.wineevents-calendar.com

www.winecountry.com

Wine Pricing

www.wine-searcher.com

www.winealert.com

Wine Tastings throughout the U.S.

www.localwineevents.com

Personalized Wine Bottles

Custom Wine Source www.customwinesource.com
(877) 862-3507

Wine Label www.winelabel.com   (800) 411-3732

International Wine Travel and Tours

Avalon Tours (worldwide) www.avalon-tours.com
(949) 673-7376

Cellar Tours (Spain and Portugal)
www.cellartours.com   (011) 34-91-521-3939

Chateau Meyre (Bordeaux, France)
wwwchateaumeyre.com (011) 33-5-56-58-10-77

Fine Wine Travel (worldwide cruise ships)
www.finewinetravel.com   (888) 208-8338

Fynbos Trails (South Africa on horseback)
www.fynbostrails.com (011) 27-82-335-8132

Gourmet Touring (Bordeaux, France via classic
convertible sports cars) www.gourmettouring.com
(011) 33-6-32-80-04-74

Shop, Wine and Dine (Italy)
www.shopwineanddine.com   (973) 467-4418

Tasting Places (Piedmont, Italy)
www.tastingplaces.com   (011) 44-208-964-5333

Food and Wine Trails Epicurean Tours
www.foodandwinetrails.com (800) 367-5348

Small Cruise Ships   www.smallshipcruises.com
(800) 290-0077

Wineries with Accommodations

USA

Bernardus Winery, Carmel Valley, CA, 57 suites.
www.bernardus.com (888) 648-9463

Clif Lede Vineyard's Poetry Inn, Napa Valley, CA,
5 deluxe rooms. www.poetryinn.com
(707) 944-0646

Fizpatrick Winery, near the Sierra Mountains, CA,
5 rooms. www.fitzpatrickwinery.com
(800) 245-9166

Keuka Overlook Inn, Dundee, NY, 4 rooms.
www.keukaoverlook.com (607) 292-6877

Prager Winery, Napa, CA, 2 rooms.
www.pragerport.com   (707) 963-3270

Rust Ridge Ranch Winery Napa, CA, 5 rooms.
www.rustridge.com (800) 788-0263

Overseas

Black Barn Vineyards, North Island of New Zealand.
7 houses. www.blackbarn.com (011) 64-6877-7985

Château de Chorey, Burgundy, France. Seventeenth-
century château complete with moat. 5 rooms and
a family suite. www.chateau-de-chorey-les-beaune.fr
(011) 33-380-22-06-05

Chateau Smith Haut Lafite's Les Sources
de Caudalie, Bordeaux, France, 49 rooms
www.sources-caudalie.com
(011) 33-5-57-83-83-83.

Domaine de la Combotte, Burgundy, France,
8 rooms. Contemporary with ultra modern
bathrooms. Outdoor pool. www.lacombotte.com.
(011) 33-380-26-02-66.

Marques de Riscal Winery, Rioja, Spain.
Frank Gehry–designed winery, spa, and hotel
with 14 rooms. www.starwoodhotels.com
(800) 325-3589

Villa Mangiacane, Tuscany, Italy. 8 suites in a
sumptuous fifteenth-century villa six miles from
Florence. (011) 39-055-829-0123
www.mangiacane.com

Index